don't panic!

pregnancy book

don't panic!
pregnancy book

tips for moms-to-be and new mothers

By Judy Morris
with forewords by Beth Iovinelli, RN, BSN,
and Jay Ugol, MD, OB/GYN

THE LYONS PRESS
Guilford, Connecticut
An imprint of The Globe Pequot Press

DISCLAIMER
The advice in this book is not intended to replace the advice of your own
healthcare practitioner. The Lyons Press, the author and editor, and contributors and their parent organizations disclaim all liability from any issue
that may arise from following the advice in this book. You and your baby
should receive regular prenatal care throughout pregnancy, assistance
during labor and delivery, and regular postnatal and pediatric care. If you
have particular questions about applying the information in this book to
your own pregnancy, speak with your own healthcare practitioner, who
can discuss your individual needs and circumstances.

The Lyons Press is an imprint of The Globe Pequot Press.

10 9 8 7 6 5 4 3 2 1

Printed in the United States of America

Designed by Carol Sawyer, Rose Design

ISBN 1-59228-353-5

Library of Congress Cataloging-in-Publication data is available on file.

Dedication

In memory of Carolyn Kelly-Wallach, a good friend and mentor who was always there for me with guidance and support when I needed her. She brought out the humor in pregnancy, and she did it with great style.

Contents

Acknowledgments   ix

Forewords   xi

Introduction   3

Eating and Drinking
for a Well Baby   8

Medicines and Health Care
for a Well Pregnancy   27

Leading a Balanced Life:
Work, Hobbies, and Pets   37

Looking Good, Feeling Great:
Bathing and Beauty Rituals   54

Changes in Your Body: Surviving the
Metamorphosis to Mom   62

Let's Go Shopping! What You
Need, What You Don't,
and Where to Put It   97

Preparing for the Big Day: A Little
Organization Goes a Long Way   116

At the Hospital: Pointers for the
Proudest (and Most Confusing)
Moments of Your Life   133

Coming Home: Self-Care for
Shell-Shocked Parents   143

Learning Your Baby's Body   162

Sane Mommy Philosophy   174

Breastfeeding 101   184

Bottle Feeding Basics   214

Envoi: Trust Yourself!   221

About the Author   224

About the Contributors   225

Index   227

Acknowledgments

You can't have a baby alone, and you can't write a book alone either!

Thanks to a little girl named Lina Hjalmarsson Lyons for planting the seed to write such a book.

Thanks to Dr. Jay Ugol and Nurse Beth Iovinelli for their meticulous care and comfort in the delivery of my son, Jimmy, and this book. Beth is as calming and reassuring with childbirth as she was throughout the writing of this book.

Thanks to Dr. Isis Bartels and Nurse Anita Soto-Ortiz, of Willows Pediatric Group in Westport, Connecticut, for taking such good care of Jimmy and me during those first tiresome and trying months.

Thanks to my editor, Susannah Hogendorn—a mother of a beautiful three-year-old girl, Isabel—for her support and excitement.

Thanks to Grandma, Grandpa, and Elizabeth Maglione for their love and babysitting! And a special thank you to my mom for her guidance, support, and especially for loving Jimmy so much.

Thanks to my husband, Jim: without his strong guidance, loving support, and endless patience, this book would not be in print.

And, last but not least, thank you, Jimmy, my beautiful baby boy. You gave me the knowledge and the courage to write this book.

Forewords

panic (*noun*) a sudden overpowering fright. *synonym*: see **fear**

Felt this before? Have you just discovered you're pregnant? Thinking about going through labor? Wondering how you'll know what to do when the baby cries?

In my more than ten years' experience as a maternal/child health nurse and lactation consultant, I've seen certain questions that consistently arise for new parents and parents-to-be. These questions start the moment you discover you are pregnant, and they continue even after the baby is born. The women and babies I meet are all very unique, but many of the fears are universal. It doesn't matter what cultural background you are from; you want to know that your baby is all right.

Becoming a parent is like starting a new job without a job description! It's a learn-as-you-go experience. Many new parents are so afraid that they'll do something wrong—or miss something—that the joy of holding, feeding, and nurturing their new child is lost in a state of panic.

One common question I get when teaching classes to new and expectant parents is, "Can I spoil my baby if I hold her too much?" Or, "Should I let her cry before I pick her up?" A well-known pediatrician named Gail Hertz, MD, IBCLC, gives some wise advice, which I share with parents in my classes. She says:

> You wonder if you should let your baby cry. Let me put it this way. Say I'm on call tonight, and I choose not to answer my beeper. After all, the vast majority of calls I get could easily wait until the office opens in the morning. A lot of them are just reassurance calls or parents who just need to talk. Say you're trying to get in touch with me. You'll probably be

frustrated, maybe a bit frightened (if you were worried), and you'd quickly come to the conclusion that you couldn't count on me when I don't answer. You'd probably even be angry enough to look for a new pediatrician. Your baby can't walk, he can't talk. He's totally dependent on you. He can't go out and look for new parents. Babies whose needs are attended to cry much less than babies who are ignored or made to wait.

By this time the parents in my classes are nodding their heads in agreement. Makes sense, right?

When a baby is born, she has been thrust into a loud, bright world full of stimulation—which, quite frankly, can be a bit much for adults. Imagine going from utter darkness, with all sound muffled, to the noise and light of the extrauterine universe! Your baby wants your reassurance. One of the first things she does is learn to establish trust with the world. By responding to her crying, you can help her feel secure and confident that her needs will be met.

So, after you have fed her, burped her, and changed her diaper, and your baby still seems fussy, hold her close; talk to her in a soft voice. Your voice is familiar to her; it will help to reassure her. Most of this should be instinctual for parents, but the barrage of advice out there can fill new parents with such fear that they hesitate to do the most basic thing: hold and reassure their baby!

Just like many of the moms I teach and take care of, Judy had a lot of questions. But as she settled into her new mothering role, I saw her relax and start to enjoy her baby. After many of her initial questions were answered, she got down to the business of parenting—and enjoying being Jimmy's mom.

As I do my job, I love seeing parents go from frightened and panicked to confident. A dad becomes a diapering pro; a mom can rattle off how often the baby should eat and how many wet diapers the baby should have. Being educated, and knowing where to look for answers, can help ease the panic when something unexpected arises. This book is a great place to start.

Beth Iovinelli, RN, BSN, IBCLC
Norwalk Hospital, Norwalk, Connecticut

When Judy Morris first asked me to help with the *Don't Panic! Pregnancy Book,* I was flattered and intrigued. I've been an obstetrician/gynecologist for eighteen years, guiding my patients through an array of different pregnancy questions and concerns. My profession brings great rewards and I enjoy supporting women through their pregnancies, and yet, I've never been involved with writing a book about it. I hope this book will offer further support to women in this exciting phase of their lives.

Written with humor and wisdom, the *Don't Panic! Pregnancy Book* eliminates needless worry and helps you to truly enjoy the journey of motherhood. Women do the greatest work of childbearing. Most of my job is reassurance and guidance. Although each pregnancy and child is unique, many of the questions I hear from my patients are the same. This book will answer many of the common questions and help alleviate some of the concerns and fears you may have, so that you can spend those valuable visits with your healthcare provider focusing on other, more specific issues.

Once a baby is born, my job is done, but this book takes you further—into the first few months of parenthood. It contains a wealth of information on both baby care and self-care. I cannot emphasize enough the importance of self-care in those early days of parenthood. Make time for yourself; follow your instincts; relax as best you can. And remember: there are thousands of healthcare professionals whose goal is to help you succeed. Don't be afraid to ask questions.

Jay Ugol, MD, OB/GYN
Norwalk Hospital, Norwalk, Connecticut

don't panic!

pregnancy book

INTRODUCTION

Congratulations, Don't Panic!

When I called my doctor's office to report that my home pregnancy test was positive, the nurse said, "Congratulations!" and asked how long it had been since my last period. I was two weeks late, so she estimated that I was six weeks pregnant! I could hardly believe it—I was already a month and a half pregnant? I'd gone from thinking that I was just a little late to being *six weeks pregnant!*

Then I panicked. *Six weeks?* What have I done in the past six weeks, I thought to myself. Let's review: I'd had a large latte every day. It was around the holidays, so I had been to more than one Christmas party, one of which served the best eggnog! I had been to my friend's bachelorette party, which went on 'til 4:00 A.M. . . . need I say more? Oh yeah: let's not forget about the dozen raw oysters I had eaten the day I took my test. The list goes on and on. . . .

I confessed it all to the nurse, who said it was OK and not to worry about it. "Just don't do it again," she instructed—which only made me worry more. What had I already done to the baby?

You are not alone if you've consumed or indulged in a few things that you wouldn't have if you'd known you were pregnant. According to Cindy Malin, a genetics counselor at Nor-walk Hospital in Norwalk, Connecticut, a woman has taken six different kinds of drugs on aver-age—including caffeine, alcohol, and aspirin—by the time she realizes she's pregnant!

But when you look at how conception really works, you'll see that there's usually less cause for concern than you think. In fact, your baby has been receiving direct nourishment from your bloodstream for only two or three weeks.

Here's a refresher course.

How It All Begins

At birth, a female human being is born with a lifelong supply of egg cells. Each month, beginning at puberty, she will release an egg cell from one of her two ovaries. This cycle is repeated, depleting her original egg supply, until she reaches menopause. Human eggs can be fertilized for only twelve to twenty-four hours; if an egg is not fertilized, it dies and leaves the body approximately two weeks later, during menstruation.

A pregnancy is counted from Day 1 of your menstrual cycle. Ovulation occurs fourteen days before you expect your next period to begin.

At conception (on or around Day 14, for a twenty-eight-day cycle) your egg is entered by a single sperm, and the miracle of new life begins. This first contact usually occurs in the fallopian tube, and the fertilized egg travels down the fallopian tube for two to seven days—until it reaches the uterus, where it's embedded into the lining. That brings us to about the third week of pregnancy, and yes, you really are pregnant at this point. But the fertilized egg takes two or three more days to develop into an embryo with a placenta and umbilical cord. Only then—between the third and fourth weeks of pregnancy—does your baby tap into your bloodstream and gain access to whatever potentially hazardous substances you've been ingesting.

The Bottom Line

The bottom line is, you haven't been bombarding your baby with potentially dangerous substances for as long as you may think. And as you'll learn in the rest of this book, for the most part, you won't need to panic during your pregnancy. So take a deep breath, clear your mind, and turn the page. Let's enjoy this baby-growing business: it will be over before you know it.

EATING AND DRINKING FOR A WELL BABY

Coffee and Caffeine

Many of us rely on the stimulating effects of coffee just to get out of bed in the morning. The good news is, you can still have that morning cup during pregnancy. But moderation is the key. What is moderate? Enjoy one good cup of coffee, then switch to decaf (keep in mind that throughout the day, you may be eating other foods that contain caffeine).

According to OTIS, the Organization of Teratology Information Services, caffeine does cross the placenta, and babies can show its effects.

CAFFEINE IN COMMON FOODS AND BEVERAGES

FOOD OR DRINK	SERVING SIZE	CAFFEINE CONTENT (MG)
Coffee	8-oz cup	65–120
Häagen-Dazs coffee ice cream	1 cup	58
Coke	12 oz	45
Brewed tea	8-oz cup	20–90
Hershey's chocolate bar	10 g	20–30

Information courtesy of the Organization of Teratology Information Services, www.otispregnancy.org

Mothers who drank excessive amounts of coffee during pregnancy delivered babies with faster heart rates, slight tremors, and unusual levels of alertness for newborns. It's best to eliminate any worries—so keep it to one cup a day and enjoy it!

What about Herbal Teas and Supplements?

If you already enjoy herbal teas or want to substitute them for coffee during pregnancy, it's essential that you consult your healthcare provider first. Some herbs, such as peppermint, are harmless. (Peppermint can even help ease indigestion.) Many herbal products aren't closely regulated by the government, so whether it's a tea or a supplement you're considering, don't take the claims on the package at face value.

Enjoying Fish and Seafood Safely

If you've been looking forward all winter long to fresh fish and clambakes on the beach, do you really have to give them up just because you're pregnant when summer arrives? *Don't panic*: the answer is a resounding "No!"

Fish is a great source of protein, low in saturated fat, and high in healthy omega-3 fatty acids. In short, it's a great part of a pregnant woman's diet. You just have to use some caution. Here, I'll explain what all the fuss is about and give you guidelines for enjoying fish and seafood safely.

Choose Cooked Fish

It's a good idea to not eat raw or rare fish during your pregnancy. If you love sushi, limit yourself to the cooked variety: California rolls, shrimp tempura, cooked eel, and so on. Most Japanese restaurants make a pregnancy roll with cooked fish. The U.S. Food and Drug Administration (FDA) says not to eat raw fish, because parasites such as worms or fluke *can* be found in raw fish. In order to kill parasites, fish must be cooked thoroughly before serving.

Stay away from raw shellfish, too. The FDA reports, "The greatest risk of seafood-borne illness is from raw or undercooked shellfish—particularly clams, oysters, and mussels from contaminated waters." The key word is _contaminated_ waters, so if you did have raw shellfish before you found out you were pregnant, it's not the end of the world. (The day I took my pregnancy test, I had eaten a huge platter of raw oysters!)

Fish and Mercury Content

Mercury is a naturally occurring mineral. When it mixes with the bacteria found in water, it transforms into methylmercury, which is toxic. Fish absorb methylmercury through their gills as they feed, and it stays in their flesh. Some types of fish absorb more methylmercury than others, and if you eat _large quantities_ of these fish, it _could_ affect your baby. (Too much exposure to methylmercury can harm your unborn child's central nervous system, which can cause slower cognitive development.) But you have to eat large quantities.

Which are the fish to avoid? According to the FDA, all women of childbearing age—whether pregnant, breastfeeding, or neither—should *avoid eating swordfish, shark, tilefish, and king mackerel.* Because these bigger fish have lived longer in the water, they've been exposed to methylmercury for a longer time and carry more of it in their flesh.

Still, "Women who had swordfish for dinner last night shouldn't panic," stresses FDA food chief Joseph Levitt. The risk comes from mercury building up, not from a single meal.

What about other types of fish? The FDA gives its approval for pregnant and nursing moms to enjoy twelve ounces per week of all the other fish in the sea, including shellfish. Depending on the serving size, that's one to three meals of seafood you can enjoy each week!

Eating Fish You've Caught

For some people, the best fish dinner is one they've caught themselves. You *can* eat your own catch if you're pregnant. Check with your local environmental and fish and wildlife agencies; they often issue fish safety advisories. If no advice is available where you are, the FDA says it's fine to eat up to six ounces per week of fish you've caught yourself, as long as you eat no other fish that week.

A Safer Tuna Sandwich

If you're a fan of tuna fish, the FDA suggests choosing canned light tuna rather than albacore ("white") tuna. Canned light tuna has less mercury. If you really love the albacore, keep your intake to one six-ounce can or less per week.

Fish and PCBs

The effects of PCBs, or polychlorinated biphenyls, aren't as well-documented as they are for mercury, so you're less likely to have heard of them. PCBs are industrial contaminants that settle in the fatty tissues of fish and other animals. Farmed salmon is of special concern because these fish may be fed fishmeal with especially high PCB concentrations. Some studies have linked PCBs to reduced birthweight, while others have suggested a link between mothers' PCB consumption and babies' motor skill and memory problems (these problems generally resolve in the long run). There is no need to panic at this point, but in case you're concerned, here are a couple of simple tips to reduce your PCB intake:

- Avoid farmed salmon.
- Since PCBs are found in the skin and fatty areas of contaminated fish, it helps to remove the skin and trim off excess fat.

- It's also a good idea to cook the fish on a rack, such as in your broiler or outside on the grill. This way, the fat will drip away from the fish, and the fish won't be cooked in it.
- PCBs can be transferred through breast milk, so if you're going to use these tips, you'll want to continue while breastfeeding.

What about Soft Cheeses and Deli Meats?

When you're pregnant, you eat a lot! At a Christmas party, I became fixated on a wheel of Brie. It was delicious, but it was also a soft cheese. Weeks later, when I first read that pregnant women should avoid soft cheeses, that wheel of Brie I had devoured came flashing back.

So, why should you not eat soft cheese? Some, but not all, soft cheeses *may* be made with unpasteurized milk, which *could* contain the bacteria called *listeria*.

Listeria can make otherwise healthy adults sick with flulike symptoms—a disease called *listeriosis*. If you became ill with listeriosis during pregnancy, it could be quite serious to your unborn child.

According to the Centers for Disease Control and Prevention (CDC), there are 2,500 cases of listeriosis a year, and you're twenty times more likely to become sick from listeria when you're pregnant. (Of the 2,500 annual listeriosis cases, one-third occur in pregnant women.) To avoid listeria during pregnancy, the CDC recommends avoiding all products made with unpasteurized milk. Since meat can also carry listeria, the CDC also adds that you should eat only thoroughly cooked meats; you should not handle cutting boards or utensils that have touched raw meat; and you should abstain from deli meats and hot dogs.

So what if you've craved and eaten Italian combos early in your pregnancy, like I did? First, *don't panic*. I figured the odds were low that my particular deli meat was contaminated. However, I also decided to avoid deli meats in the future. If you want more reassurance, talk to your health-care provider. A blood culture can tell whether you're carrying the listeria bacteria.

As for the cheese lovers among us, most cheeses in the United States are made from pas-teurized milk, but it doesn't hurt to ask before buying if it's not clearly marked on the package. Also, you'll need to be extra-vigilant when trav-eling abroad. Hard cheeses, cream cheese, cot-tage cheese, and yogurt are all listeria-free and are very good for a pregnant woman's diet.

Morning Sickness: When Food Repels You

"Morning sickness" can occur morning, noon, and night, and it's very common. "Morning sick-ness is related to the rapid rise in the hormone called HCG, which peaks around eight to twelve weeks and settles down between sixteen and twenty weeks," says Jay Ugol, MD, an ob-stetrician/gynecologist at Norwalk Hospital in

Connecticut. "The hormone HCG is produced by the placenta, not the fetus. Therefore, a woman may experience stronger morning sickness with twins, because she has two placentas."

If you are sick for your entire pregnancy, your morning sickness could have another cause: it could be because your uterus is pushing on your stomach and diaphragm.

Don't panic if you're so nauseated that the thought of eating anything healthy makes you feel ill. You shouldn't downplay the importance of nutrition in the first trimester, but if you're so sick that the only thing you can stomach is saltines and ginger ale, your baby will still be fine. During the first nine to ten weeks, the fetus and the organs are being formed, and in these beginning weeks of pregnancy, all babies are basically the same size. It's in the later months that they reach different sizes. It's at *that* time, in the second trimester and beyond, that your baby begins to put on weight. By then you'll hopefully be feeling better, and food will seem more appealing.

While you're feeling sick, try eating small, frequent meals that include plenty of complex carbohydrates and are high in protein.

Quell Queasiness with Vinegar

My local health food store recommended that I try a little apple cider vinegar mixed with water, and it really did make my nausea much better. Try adding 1 teaspoon of apple cider vinegar to eight ounces of water, and adjust it to your liking by adding more water to make it weaker or more vinegar to make it stronger.

Eat Your Way through Morning Sickness

- Eat a dry or plain muffin or crackers for breakfast.
- Drink plenty of fluids, one sip at a time, if that's all you can tolerate.
- Eat small amounts often.

- Ginger is very soothing to the stomach. Make a stir-fry with ginger, or look for ginger capsules at your local health food store. (Be sure to check with your healthcare provider before taking any new supplements.)
- Vitamin B6 can safely help alleviate nausea and vomiting, according to the American College of OB/GYN.
- If you are really miserable, talk with your healthcare provider. Some prescription anti-nausea medications are safe to use during pregnancy.

Vitamins and Pregnancy

Stomaching Your Prenatal Vitamins

Don't worry if you're so nauseated with morning sickness that you can't even stomach your prenatal vitamin. The iron it contains may aggravate

your morning sickness. It helps to take the vitamin with food or right before you go to bed.

The sheer size of your multivitamin can also
present a problem. Wouldn't you think, in this
high-tech age, they'd come up with a way to
make vitamins smaller? Until then, if the size of
your vitamin is making you gag, chop it up and
take it with a teaspoon of jelly.

My friend Cristiane was especially sensitive to her vitamins—they made her feel sicker
than she already was. "My morning sickness
was so bad, I couldn't even swallow my prenatal vitamin," she says. "I was worried that my
baby would not get all the proper vitamins, but
my doctor reassured me that if I ate a balanced, healthy diet before getting pregnant
that a healthy foundation was already set. My
doctor even suggested trying Flintstones vitamins. It helped because I didn't have to swallow a big pill."

If you can't stomach any vitamin at all, just
try to eat a healthy diet and make sure to include

foods that are rich in folic acid, a supplement form that's added to many breakfast cereals, or folate, the naturally occurring form of the vitamin. It helps to prevent neural tube defects, and pregnant women should have at least 800 micrograms per day. (Ideally, you should start this intake prior to conception, but if you haven't, don't worry; your child's risk of neural tube defects is not increased.) Good natural sources of folate include blueberries, papaya, dark leafy greens, chickpeas and lentils, and wheat germ.

Keeping an Eye on Vitamin A

I thought *all* vitamins during pregnancy would be great for the baby. So, every day, I went to my local health food store and drank a fresh glass of carrot juice. Then, I read that vitamin A in excessive amounts could cause birth defects.

In order not to panic, you need to understand that there are two types of vitamin A. The first is beta-carotene, a natural substance found in fruits and vegetables that converts to the good kind of vitamin A in the body, which is okay during pregnancy. (So you can have that carrot juice every day!)

The second type of vitamin A is retinol esters—a synthetic form. The U.S. Recommended Daily allowance of vitamin A as retinol esters is 8,000 IU. Other studies suggest that pregnant women keep their intake of this form of vitamin A to less than 4,000 IU. Retinol esters can be found in vitamins, in fortified foods, and in many popular facial creams, so check with your doctor before continuing use of such products.

Don't be extreme and limit all vitamin A from your diet. It's a required vitamin for a healthy pregnancy. Just continue to take your daily multivitamin, and eat foods that contain the natural form of beta-carotene. Be aware of energy bars and cereals that are heavily fortified—they can sometimes contain the equivalent of a multivitamin.

Artificial Sweeteners: Are They Safe?

When you get into the habit of reading food labels, you'll be amazed at how many different types of foods use artificial sweeteners. It's not just in diet sodas! According to the U.S. Food and Drug Administration, aspartame, which is found in Nutrasweet and Equal, appears to be safe during pregnancy. (Of course, it should be taken in moderation, as part of a healthy diet.)

Splenda, another type of sweetener, is a modification of regular table sugar—only about 600 times sweeter! Again, if you use it in moderation and eat healthfully overall, there are no studies suggesting that it is dangerous to your unborn child.

Saccharin, however, should be avoided. It can cross the placenta and remain in the fetal tissue. Some scientists think it may actually remain in the baby's bladder, which in later years could cause bladder cancer. But *don't panic* if you've had a few foods that contain saccharin; small amounts early on in the pregnancy are not going to cause any harm.

MEDICINES AND HEALTH CARE FOR A WELL PREGNANCY

Getting the Best from Your Healthcare Provider

Navigating our modern healthcare system can be really frustrating. But it can also be extremely fulfilling. Pregnancy and childbirth are a prime example: your healthcare provider will be your partner through the whole experience, so be sure to pick someone you like and trust.

Will you choose an obstetrician or a midwife? Where will you deliver? Do you mind seeing more than one person (in a group practice)? Don't be scared to shop around and ask other mothers for recommendations. And above all, *don't be afraid to ask questions,* no matter how silly you think they may be. You'll have lots of them when you're choosing a healthcare provider, and throughout the rest of your pregnancy. (This goes for choosing your baby's pediatrician, too.)

What kinds of answers can you expect to your medical questions? "It's recommended . . ." "It's preferred . . ." "It should be avoided . . ." "The risk appears to be . . ." "It's reasonable to be cautious . . ." "It's cause for concern . . ." If you haven't already heard these vague phrases, you soon will! Getting a straight, simple answer to a medical question can be like pulling teeth. But keep in mind that it's not your healthcare provider's fault! For many of our concerns during pregnancy, there simply isn't enough scientific information for practitioners to give us concrete answers. Many of the life choices you make during pregnancy really are up to you.

What you *can* expect is a practitioner who will take you seriously, return your phone calls, and help to allay unnecessary fears. You'll get the best results if you keep up your end of the bargain by making a list of questions beforehand and taking notes at the appointment if you need to. Cultivate an atmosphere of mutual respect—you'll be glad you did.

Asserting Yourself with Experts

You'll meet many different medical experts during your pregnancy—especially if you're in a larger OB/GYN practice where you rotate through doctors. With all the different personalities, you may have the occasional bad experience. Maybe a doctor or nurse simply answers your questions too quickly or in a manner that you don't understand. If that happens, don't feel shy. Remember, this is your baby and your body! Educate yourself by asking more questions until you understand.

Pills and Pregnancy

Safe Meds in Pregnancy

Always consult with your healthcare provider before taking any medications, whether you're pregnant or breastfeeding. When you are pregnant and you ingest a drug—whether it's alcohol, medication, or caffeine—it will go into your bloodstream and then pass into the placenta. Below is a quick list of medications that my doctor approved for pregnancy. Again, check with your healthcare provider to find out what's best for you—there are many others that are also safe.

Pregnancy-Safe Medicines

Here's a list of medications that are generally safe to take for occasional discomfort during pregnancy. Ask your provider what's best for you particularly if your symptoms last more than a week.

- For headaches, general aches and muscle pains, and fever: Tylenol or Extra-Strength Tylenol
- For insomnia: Tylenol PM or Benadryl
- For a cold, allergy symptoms, or sinus congestion: Sudafed, Benadryl, Afrin nasal spray, or Tylenol Sinus
- For coughing: plain Robitussin (the kind with no letters in the name)
- For a sore throat: cough drops
- For gas or indigestion: Tums, liquid Mylanta, or Maalox

"What If I Got Pregnant on the Pill?"

It can happen! While I was writing this book, a number of women told me that they were taking birth control pills when they discovered they were pregnant. They all have beautiful, healthy babies, and if this is a concern of yours, *don't panic.*

"Birth control pills are among the most studied medications since their debut in 1960," explains Moriah Ritson, Director of Medical Services for Planned Parenthood of Connecticut. "It is well accepted in the medical community that even when birth control pills are taken early in a pregnancy, there is no increased risk for birth defects. A woman who inadvertently took pills prior to or soon after she conceived should not panic."

Medical Equipment

X-Rays

The first rule of X-ray exposure is that you should avoid it if it's not absolutely necessary. However, if you must have an X-ray, be sure to tell anyone ordering an X-ray that you are pregnant; they should always use a shield to protect your belly.

What if you've recently been to the dentist and had a routine X-ray, and you didn't know you were pregnant? *Don't panic:* you were exposed to very low levels of radiation. You can call and ask the dentist or healthcare provider for extra reassurance.

What kinds of risks does your baby incur from radiation during pregnancy? Radiation exposure in the first trimester exhibits an all-or-none phenomenon, says Jay Ugol, MD, meaning that there's a slight increased risk of miscarriage but otherwise no harm. If high doses of radiation are used in the second or third trimester, there may be a slight increased chance of later leukemia.

Ultrasounds

When I was pregnant with my son, I was even worried about whether or not an ultrasound could hurt my baby! Even though it was administered by my doctor in a medical office . . . could this procedure do damage? The answer is no!

Ultrasounds are completely safe, says Jay Ugol, MD. "No test has been more scrutinized for its safety, because of its frequency of use.

There is no evidence of birth defects or developmental delays with ultrasound."

The effects of three-dimensional ultrasound are still under investigation.

Illness and Pregnancy

Flu Shots

Not only is it safe to get a flu shot when you're pregnant, it's actually a good idea, says the Advisory Committee on Immunization Practices (ACIP) of the U.S. Centers for Disease Control and Prevention. Out of 2,000 pregnant women who received the flu shot (a.k.a. the influenza vaccine), none of their newborn babies had any ill effects from the vaccine. Many medical experts believe it's safe to administer the flu shot at any point in pregnancy, including the first trimester. It isn't a live-virus vaccine, and, therefore, severe adverse reactions are rare; also, the impact of serious flu during the earliest part of pregnancy can outweigh the risk of adverse reactions.

"Help! My Shots Aren't Up to Date!"

You may not be able to recall whether all your shots are up to date, but your healthcare provider can tell from your prenatal bloodwork. Ideally, you should have these tests before you've conceived. But if you discover after conception (like I did!) that you're not up to date, you need to avoid anyone who is sick with chicken pox, measles, mumps, or German measles (also called rubella).

Chicken pox is a live vaccine, so you can't be immunized for it during your pregnancy. Most adults are immune to chicken pox anyway, even if they have no history of having the illness or of being immunized against it. A simple blood test can tell you whether you're immune. If this is your first child and you're not immune, you're at less risk of exposure to chicken pox, because you're probably not around children all the time. But it's still a good idea to tell your friends with kids that you're pregnant and you need to avoid chicken pox. If you already have a child, or if you work around children, you'll have to be a little more careful.

Once your baby is born, you can—and should—have the vaccinations you're missing. Talk to your healthcare provider about scheduling the shots. I was so busy that I forgot to schedule my chicken pox vaccination; it was only when I was trying for our second child that I remembered! To my disappointment, the chicken pox vaccine was a two-series shot with a waiting time of one month in between; plus, doctors advise waiting three months *after* the shots are given to try and conceive because the shot uses a live virus. You also need to wait one month between MMR (measles/mumps/rubella) shots, so be prepared and get your shots well in advance before thinking of a second baby.

LEADING A BALANCED LIFE: WORK, HOBBIES, AND PETS

Dealing with Panic at Work
Keeping Stress at Bay

Let's face it, our lives are becoming more and more stressful. I continued to work in a hectic environment up until the day my water broke. Light exercise every day—such as walking, meditating, and yoga—helped me balance my stress, and it will help you, too. Pregnancy can be such a wild ride, but it's a lot easier when you take time to care for yourself mentally as well as physically. And it's also good for your growing baby!

"The Baby Is Stealing My Brain Cells!"

Your baby is not stealing your brain cells, although it may feel that way sometimes! Your inability to remember, concentrate, and multitask is temporary. You just have a lot on your mind. Notes can help you feel more organized, and not just at work. Take notes at the healthcare provider's office and at childbirth classes, and be sure to write down any questions you have in between visits. You can also bring your husband, partner, or friend along: it helps to have an extra pair of ears.

Office Equipment Insanity

The instant I found out I was pregnant, I started approaching all office equipment with caution: I used to dodge the light from the microwave as it popped my popcorn (the salt and dry popcorn seemed to help my morning sickness); I avoided the photocopier's ray of light as it flashed back and forth; the buzz of my computer freaked me out; and I used to talk on my cell phone, holding it as far away from my ear as possible! The bad news is that you can stay at work; the good news is that it's all *safe*—even the metal detector at the airport.

Around the House

Painting Projects

One Saturday afternoon, I decided to paint an old piece of furniture that I had found at a tag sale. A week later, I found out I was pregnant, and that painting job went directly onto my list of worries! I was reassured by my doctor that one afternoon of painting would cause absolutely no harm to my developing baby. But I was also advised that I should probably take a break from painting tag sale finds. If you have to paint before the baby's arrival, here are some tips.

Tips for Safe Painting

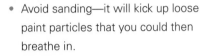

- Avoid sanding—it will kick up loose paint particles that you could then breathe in.
- Wear a mask.
- Use high-quality latex paint.
- Paint in a well-ventilated area and keep all of the windows open.
- If your project requires a more potent product, such as a paint stripper, leave that job to someone else.

Art Safety

Artists need to be especially cautious about their materials during pregnancy. For instance, some oil paints contain lead, and some solvents used for cleaning and thinning contain organic compounds that can cause birth defects. Likewise, some photography chemicals aren't good for develop-

ing babies. If you're artistically inclined, ask
your healthcare provider what's best for you
and the baby.

***

Cleaning Products

If you were looking forward to taking nine
months off from cleaning the house, sorry: you
don't have to! There are many alternatives to tra-
ditional cleaning products; check your supermar-
ket and healthfood store shelves. The American
Pregnancy Association says that common cleaning products are safe to use during pregnancy.
They do offer a few guidelines, though:

- Use proper ventilation and protect your
  skin with gloves.
- Read all labels and *never mix chemicals*—
  it can create dangerous fumes.
- Avoid cleaning areas with poor ventilation,
  such as ovens and small shower stalls.

The Safest Household Cleaner of All

Don't underestimate the power of vinegar! You can make your own safe and effective household cleaning solution from one part white vinegar and one part water. Keep it in a spray bottle and use it in the kitchen and bathroom. It even serves as a mild disinfectant if you let it sit on a surface for ten minutes before wiping. Just be sure not to mix it with bleach, as the combination produces toxic fumes.

Yuck! Dealing with Mouse Droppings

Mouse droppings in my kitchen were a disgusting surprise when I moved into a new house at two months pregnant. I remembered hearing about *hantavirus*, a respiratory disease transmitted through mouse droppings and urine, and, of course, I worried about having mice in my kitchen. As usual, though, there was *no need to panic!*

Hantavirus is extremely rare: the Centers for Disease Control and Prevention (CDC) has reported only about a hundred cases in the United States since 1993. But since the disease can be quite serious, I checked with the CDC about how to clean the droppings. They recommend spraying the affected area with a 10 percent solution of chlorine bleach and letting it sit for thirty minutes. Then, using rubber gloves, wipe down the area and throw out the rags with the mouse droppings. I gave this lovely job to my husband: when you're pregnant, why put yourself through the extra worry?

Taking It Outside

Wearing Bug Spray

DEET is the active ingredient in most insect and tick repellents. If you misuse insect repellent—

for instance, by using a whole bottle during one outing—DEET can adversely affect the central nervous system. If used properly, on the other hand, there are no known adverse side effects.

According to the Organization of Teratology Information Services, when DEET products are applied to the skin, only 10 percent of DEET passes into the bloodstream. There are conflicting views on how much, if any, is passed through the placenta to the fetus. If you're in an area where you are vulnerable to Lyme disease, West Nile virus, malaria, or yellow fever, it is a much safer bet to go with the bug spray than to risk the consequences of a serious disease.

To alleviate any worries, limit your use of products containing DEET, wear long sleeves and pants when outdoors, and place the repellent on your clothes and not your skin. Organic repellents are available that contain citronella oil instead of DEET. Ask your doctor to review the ingredients.

Protecting Yourself Against Lyme Disease

According to the American Lyme Disease Foundation, deer ticks, carried by deer and mice, are slowly spreading Lyme disease along the upper East Coast and inland, as well as through the upper Midwest and along the coasts of northern California and Oregon. For pregnant women, the effects of Lyme disease on the fetus are still unknown, and transmission of the disease from mother to fetus seems to be rare. If you are bitten, look for a telltale bull's-eye or red blotch around the bite. The average rash is five to six inches in diameter, but it can be bigger or smaller or located elsewhere. If you have it, see a healthcare provider right away. "Lyme disease should be treated with three weeks of oral amoxicillin, which is safe during pregnancy," says Jay Ugol, MD.

To help prevent Lyme disease:

- Keep your lawn short, and remove old leaf litter, brush, and woodpiles.
- Stay out of brushy areas. If you like to hike, wear a long-sleeve shirt and long pants tucked into boots. It helps if your clothing is light-colored—it's easier to see the ticks. For added protection, you can apply DEET products to your clothing.
- Do a "tick check" on yourself and your family each night during tick season (from the last frost in the spring, until the first frost in the fall). It takes twenty-four to forty-eight hours after the tick has embedded itself for the disease to pass into your system. Closely inspect your skin and scalp, paying special attention to body creases. Deer ticks are tiny.

Your Lawn and Garden

What to do with those weeds in the yard—let them grow, or treat them with chemicals? When you're pregnant, it's always best to avoid chemicals. When I was pregnant, my biggest backyard concern was Lyme disease, not weeds. I asked my doctor if it was OK to treat the yard. And it is, with a couple of caveats: you shouldn't be outside when the chemicals are being applied, and you shouldn't sit directly on the grass until a couple of hours have passed. Always check first with the company that is doing the work; it can give you specific guidelines to match the product it's using. You may want to consider organic lawn treatments: though they may also require caution, they're better for the environment, and that benefits your family in the long run.

Wear Gardening Gloves

It's best to wear gloves while gardening when you're pregnant. There's a slight chance garden soil can harbor *Toxoplasma gondii,* a parasite that can cause mild illness in mothers and more serious problems in unborn babies. (See page 49 for more on Toxoplasma.)

Will Loud Music Hurt the Baby?

Don't miss a good concert just because you're pregnant! An occasional concert or two will not harm your unborn baby. After the twenty-fourth week of pregnancy, your baby can hear sounds from the outside world, but your amniotic fluid helps to muffle the high-pitched noises.

Your Multi-Species Family

Cleaning Your Cat's Litter Box

People may have told you that your cat's litter box can be dangerous to your unborn child. This is because of *Toxoplasma gondii,* a parasite that can make you sick and cause infection in your baby. Toxoplasma gondii can be found in undercooked meat and raw eggs, as well as in an infected cat's feces. But a certain chain of events has to happen for your cat to become infected. She has to eat infected raw meat or an infected rodent—and even then, the parasite only lives in her feces for two to three weeks.

According to the U.S. Centers for Disease Control and Prevention, there are medications to treat toxoplasmosis when you're pregnant, but careful monitoring is a must, even after birth. To be on the safe side, you really should give the litter-box job to some other family member for the duration of your pregnancy. If you absolutely have to do it, wear gloves and a mask, as toxoplasmosis can become airborne when the dusty kitty litter is disturbed. Always wash your hands with warm, soapy water when you're done.

Preparing Your Pets for the Baby

Soon after my husband and I first met, we fell madly in love with a dog. He was a skinny, nine-month-old boxer puppy who had been rescued from an abusive family. He needed a lot of TLC—and we gave him so much that we've always considered him our first child. Later, we decided to get a second boxer from the ASPCA. All was well in the family until the dogs reached adolescence and started to fight. We managed them carefully and understood that we had taken on a huge responsibility living with two aggressive male dogs. But when I became pregnant, the hushed whispers and wary exchanges between our friends and family began: "What are you going to do with the dogs once the baby arrives?" "You're not going to keep them . . . are you?"

Well, we couldn't bear the thought of getting rid of them, so, "Yes," we told our concerned friends, "We *are* going to keep them." And we started preparing right away.

I consulted with numerous experts and spent a lot of time on lessons and advice. Here are some of the things we did to prepare our dogs for the baby:

- I bought a CD of a newborn baby's cries, gurgles, and squeals. I played it over and over so the sounds would become familiar. I don't know who was more uneasy with the loud cries: my husband or the dogs. The tape worked on both, though!
- I outfitted the baby's room as soon as possible, so the "boys" could get used to the new furniture and smells.

- I purchased a lifelike doll that cried and cooed, and I wore the doll in a baby sling around the house. I also put the doll in the carriage, leashed both dogs, and took them for walks with the crying "baby." As we walked down the street, I periodically threw treats, praising the dogs for their good behavior. I'd give them extra praise after tough maneuvers, such as turning the baby carriage around and into their feet.
- We prepared well in advance for any changes in the dogs' routine that we could anticipate (fewer walks around the block, less freedom in the house, less attention, no more sleeping on our bed . . .). That way, the dogs couldn't blame negative changes on the baby. (By the way, this advice also works on husbands!)

When the baby was born, my husband brought home a dirty diaper and some worn Onesies from the hospital, so the dogs could get used to the new smell. On homecoming day, my husband greeted both dogs first, while I held the baby; then I greeted the dogs while he held the baby. Finally, after we'd both greeted the dogs, we introduced the baby.

What an uneventful event that was: one sniff and a little lick, and they were off to their dog beds. Would that have been the case without all the training? Who knows . . . but we weren't going to take the chance.

LOOKING GOOD, FEELING GREAT: BATHING AND BEAUTY RITUALS

Bathing for Relaxation and Health

Before I got pregnant, I loved nothing more than to take a nice, long bath at the end of a stressful day. A warm bath is a soothing way to relax, and if you're a bath lover, chances are you may have had a few long soaks before finding out that you were pregnant.

Here's some good news: you can continue to enjoy warm baths up until your water breaks, as long as the water isn't too hot.

What's too hot? As a general rule, you should be able to slip right into the water without inching in little by little. You should not experience sweating, your skin turning red, or mild wooziness.

Once your water has broken, medical professionals have varying opinions about whether or not you should immerse yourself in water. Check with your healthcare provider.

What About Hot Tubs and Saunas?

A normal, healthy body temperature is around 98.6°F. Sitting in a hot tub or a sauna for more than ten minutes can raise your body temperature to 102°F.

A raised body temperature, from an illness or excessive heat, in the first eight weeks of pregnancy can be dangerous to the fetus's neural tube (the neural tube becomes the spinal cord). The neural tube is not completely closed until the eighth week of pregnancy. Once the tube is closed, according to the Organization of Teratology Information Services (OTIS), your baby is no longer at risk for neural tube disorders.

So, after your eight-week mark, it's up to you whether to indulge in hot tubs and saunas. Just keep it to less than ten minutes, and be sure to stay hydrated by drinking plenty of water.

Skin Care and Pregnancy

Pregnancy-Induced Acne

Many of us have been agonizing over pimples since adolescence. For other women, pregnancy can bring on a sudden case of acne. Don't panic; it's just your overactive hormones, which can make you produce too much *sebum* (the oil that normally just keeps your skin supple). Too much sebum leads to blocked pores and pimples. Once the baby comes, your hormones will start to calm down and your sebum production will slow down. In the meantime, wash your face often, use a noncomedogenic (non-pore-blocking) moisturizer, and think positively—women with oilier skin have fewer wrinkles! Check with your doctor before applying medicated acne cream.

If You've Been Using Retin-A

Retin-A is a miracle cream that many dermatologists prescribe for acne and other skin conditions. For women who rely on it, giving it up during pregnancy can be a tough choice to make. So I asked Sherri Kaplan, MD, a dermatologist in Ardsley, New York, whether it was really necessary to stop using Retin-A during pregnancy. She advises, "When you're pregnant, it's always best to be conservative, so yes, stop using Retin-A.

You can begin using it again after you deliver—you'll get right back to your prepregnancy skin in no time at all."

Don't panic, however, if you used Retin-A before you knew you were pregnant. The Organization of Teratology Information Services (OTIS) explains that if you apply Retin-A cream to your skin, only about 10 percent of the active ingredient will pass into your bloodstream, and even less will reach the baby.

Self-Tanning Creams

Who doesn't like to have a golden tan? If you've relied on tanning creams to achieve such a look, you don't need to panic because you're pregnant. Very little, if any, tanning cream is absorbed through your skin and into your bloodstream, so you haven't harmed your baby. But it's best to limit your use—there simply hasn't been enough research to establish whether they're absolutely safe for use during pregnancy.

Lotions with Alpha Hydroxy

Alpha hydroxy is an ingredient found in skin creams and lotions. It gently exfoliates and leaves your skin with a rosy glow. But it may leave you a little too rosy when you're pregnant. "During pregnancy," says dermatologist Sherri Kaplan, "your skin can be very sensitive, so it's best to stay away from products that contain alpha hydroxy. They can be very irritating. Instead, choose products that are mild and fragrance-free." Alpha hydroxy can also pass through your skin, with effects that aren't completely known.

The silver lining here is that soon, you won't need face creams to give you a rosy glow. If you don't have one yet, you will! I felt tired and pale for the first few months of my pregnancy; but later, when lots of extra blood was pumping through my body, I really was radiant.

Coloring, Perming, and Straightening Your Hair

Pregnant women often ask about the safety of hair coloring. To color or not to color? How about a highlight or two? And what about perms and straighteners?

The bottom line on any healthcare or beauty treatment—whether it's highlighting, permanent color, or permanents or body waves—is this: most of the companies who make these products don't have the resources for extensive research and studies in pregnancy. Instead, they advise you to consult a physician before use. What is a physician to say, without proper research and testing? "During pregnancy, no matter what you are exposed to, there is an underlying risk of birth defects of 2 to 5 percent. We do not know if these products increase these underlying risks, so, if it doesn't need to be done, don't do it," says Jay Ugol, MD.

Don't panic, though, if you just had your hair processed. "If a pregnant patient were to come to me who had already colored her hair, I would certainly reassure her that her baby should not be harmed," says Dr. Ugol. "But if a pregnant woman came to me seeking permission to color her hair, I would ask her to hold off until after she had the baby."

Whitening Your Teeth

Everyone likes a bright smile, but I recommend waiting to bleach your teeth until after the baby is born and you're finished breastfeeding. Most experts feel that bleaching your teeth is *probably* safe, but there just isn't enough information to say for sure. Whether you're considering an over-the-counter product, peroxide, or even microabrasion (which uses acid), it's simply best to wait.

CHANGES IN YOUR BODY: SURVIVING THE METAMORPHOSIS TO MOM

What's Going On Down There?

Spotting Early in Pregnancy

Spotting in the first trimester is fairly common. In fact, one-third of all women experience it, and most of these women have normal, healthy pregnancies. In the very early stages of pregnancy, as the fertilized egg implants into the uterine lining, there can be a day or two of light bleeding called *implantation bleeding.* Still, it's advised that any bleeding or cramping be evaluated by ultrasound—or by hormone levels, if it's too early in the pregnancy for ultrasound.

Vaginal Discharge

Aside from spotting, many women notice a thin, whitish discharge in early pregnancy. It can progress to a thicker discharge later in pregnancy. *Don't panic*—this is perfectly normal. At the very end of pregnancy, when your baby "drops" into your pelvis, the discharge will get heavier. You may also pass the brownish mucus plug that's been covering your cervix and protecting your baby. Passage of the plug, and the pinkish bloody "show" that may follow, are signs that your cervix is dilating. Although it may still take a few weeks, your baby is on his way!

If you're concerned about changes in the color or heaviness of your vaginal discharge, call your healthcare provider. Discharge should not have an odor or be accompanied by pain, irritation, or itching.

Yeast Infections

If you have yeast infections from time to time, you know that it's nothing more than an inconvenience. Yeast infections are ten times more likely to occur when you're pregnant because of the increased level of estrogen in your system. If you think you have a yeast infection, notify your healthcare provider before purchasing a drug store remedy. "Over-the-counter yeast treatments such as Monistat and Gyne-Lotrimin that have been around for a long time and have been properly tested are perfectly safe to use during pregnancy," says Jay Ugol, MD. Still, your doctor may want to suggest a specific brand and regimen.

Sexual Intercourse during Pregnancy

It's always safest to check with your healthcare provider, but as long as you have a normal,

healthy pregnancy, you can enjoy having intercourse until the day your baby arrives! The only
restrictions are for undiagnosed vaginal bleeding, known placenta previa (where the placenta
covers the cervix), premature labor, ruptured
membranes, and premature cervical dilation.

Kegel Exercises for Better Sex

Kegel exercises are great for improving
the tone of your pubococcygeal (PC) or
pelvic floor muscles, both before and after
delivery. Good PC muscle tone makes it
easier to push during labor, it improves
your urinary continence, and it even makes
sex more pleasurable. Kegel exercises are
easy to do: imagine you have to urinate,
but you stop the stream in midflow. Hold
those muscles a few seconds, release,
then repeat.

Your Pregnant Breasts

The agony, the ecstasy . . . What woman hasn't obsessed over her breasts at some point in pregnancy? "Are mine big enough for breastfeeding?" "Whose are these, Pamela Anderson's?" "Why are my nipples changing colors?"

Don't panic. Changes in your breasts *are* the norm during pregnancy. And yes, no matter what their size, you'll be able to breastfeed if you want to. (For more information, see page 71.) For now, here's a look at the pre-delivery side of the mountain(s).

Changes in Your Breasts During Pregnancy

"Will I be able to produce milk?" This is a very common concern among new moms. Rest assured, your body has been preparing for feeding your baby long before you started to worry about it.

Your breasts begin to change in the first trimester. They grow larger because of the increased amount of glandular tissue, and they become more sensitive, too. You'll probably feel at least a slight tingling; some women grow so sore that they can't stand to be touched for a while. You may also notice your nipples and the areolas (the skin around your nipple) darkening, which is Mother Nature's way of attracting your baby.

Bumps along your areolas are another common pregnancy development. They release an oil to help lubricate and protect your nipples from any infections while you are breastfeeding.

And how about those veins? A rich supply of blood in your breasts can cause the blood vessels beneath your skin to dilate, and voilà: large blue veins. Not to worry; they'll disappear soon after the baby is born.

While all these changes are occurring, the developing placenta is stimulating the release of prolactin, a pregnancy hormone that begins the lactation process, and your breasts begin to develop milk ducts.

You can now rest assured: your body is completely prepared for breastfeeding by the second trimester!

Inverted Nipples

If you have inverted nipples, not to worry—you can still breastfeed. There are a few things you can do to help ensure that your breastfeeding experience is positive and successful. First, make sure your healthcare provider examines your nipples during checkups. Second, wear a breast shield inside your bra during your last few months of pregnancy: it places gentle pressure around the areola, gently drawing out the nipple. Third, get in touch with a lactation consultant for further support and advice before your baby arrives. Lactation consultants are an invaluable source of support for every breastfeeding mother. There may be one on staff at your hospital, or you can contact La Leche League (online at www.laleche league.org, or call 1-800-LALECHE).

"I Had Breast Surgery. Can I Still Breastfeed?"

Breast surgery—for augmentation or reduction—is becoming more common every year. *Don't panic* if you've had one of these surgeries and wish you could breastfeed. Talk to your surgeon, enlist the help of a certified lactation consultant, and prepare yourself with the following facts.

If you have implants, you may experience increased or decreased nipple sensation, or exaggerated engorgement. Depending on how the surgery was done, it could impact your milk supply.

If you've had a breast reduction, be aware that some moms make a lot of milk, while others have a marginal supply. This is a multifaceted issue. Research, talk to others, and learn as much as possible to increase your chances of success. Beth Iovinelli, a registered maternal/child nurse and lactation consultant at Norwalk Hospital in Connecticut, recommends reading *Defining Your Own Success* by Diana West (La Leche League

International, 2001). Also check out the Breast-feeding After Reduction website at www.bfar.org.

Leaking Nipples

Don't be alarmed if one day you notice your nipples leaking a thick, yellowish fluid. If this fluid dries on your nipples, it may appear that you have an infection. I thought I did, and I ran right to the doctor. After having my nipples examined, I was relieved to hear that it was actually good news! My breasts were doing their job: they were producing *colostrum,* and it's normal for a little to leak during pregnancy. (If your nipples are leaking any blood, they should be checked.)

Colostrum is a thick, creamy, sometimes yellow fluid that contains antibodies and is high in protein. The breast begins producing this pre-milk at around sixteen weeks of pregnancy. You can be reassured that your breasts are in working order and are on their way to becoming full-fledged milk producing machines!

Does Breast Size Matter for Milk Production?

The answer is: not at all. What makes a pre-pregnancy breast large is the amount of fat. Fat does not create milk. Milk-producing tissues are what make milk, and those are developed during your pregnancy. Even if your breasts aren't large at the end of your pregnancy, you can feed your baby just as well as a woman who wears a double-D!

Dealing with Exhaustion and Fatigue

You can never fully prepare for how tired you'll feel during pregnancy and new motherhood. During the first trimester, many women feel a chronic sense of fatigue. This dissipates during the second trimester, when a burst of excitement and energy tends to kick in. Then comes the third trimester: your growing belly makes sleeping increasingly uncomfortable; and when you throw in the frequent trips to the bathroom, you can say goodbye to a good night's sleep.

Tips for Coping with Exhaustion

During pregnancy:

- During your third trimester, try sleeping with extra pillows or a body pillow to help support your stomach.
- To reduce the nighttime trips to the bathroom, drink plenty of water during the day, but keep it to a minimum just before bed.
- Exercise for at least twenty minutes a day. Walking, swimming, and yoga are great exercises for a pregnant woman.
- Before going to bed, relax in a bath or listen to a meditation tape.

With a newborn:

- I have yet to meet the woman who can do this, but try to sleep when your baby is sleeping. A rested mother is a better mother.
- Try different sleeping arrangements with your baby, and stick to the one that works best—whether it's a crib, a bassinet, or even your own bed.
- Ask your husband or partner for his support and understanding, and "warn" him of your mood swings so he's not surprised when they occur.
- *Don't worry about how the house looks*. We all love visiting our friends who have new babies, and do we care if there are piles of dishes and clothes everywhere? Of course not! Just let it go.

Maybe this is nature's way of preparing you for the nighttime feedings to come. In the first couple of months, they can range from every hour, on the hour, to the perfect (rare) newborn who sleeps six hours straight. I was in a complete state of shock when my son's pediatrician told me that for babies less than a year old, five hours a night is considered sleeping through the night! There were times when I just didn't know how I could physically go on. Exhaustion makes simple tasks seem almost impossible.

Is there any good news here? Well, your body does seem to adjust to your new sleeping patterns, and if you were a sleeper, like me, you will be surprised at how little sleep you can get by on.

Panic Attacks and Palpitations

I never would have thought that panic attacks could be a symptom of pregnancy, but it happened to me! I was seven months pregnant and out to dinner, when all of a sudden, I felt my heart jump and my pulse race. Of course, being pregnant and panicky anyway, I thought for sure there was something wrong. My doctor wanted to be cautious, so he had me wear a Holter monitor for a few days. As fast as the symptoms came on, though, they disappeared.

Some women have heart palpitations during pregnancy, and these often disappear, too. Your healthcare provider may ask you to log them to see how often they occur. If you have chest pain or difficulty breathing, call your healthcare provider.

Your Changing Weight

Weight Gain

The basic rule of weight gain is to gain one pound per month during the first trimester, and then slightly less than one pound per week for the rest of the pregnancy. Twenty-five to thirty pounds is a nice, average weight to gain. I ended up gaining forty pounds . . . but some women only gain twenty! Bottom line: the amount of weight you put on during pregnancy is as individual as each baby. As long as you continue to eat a healthy, well-balanced diet, you are doing everything just right.

Weight Loss

Is it possible to be pregnant and actually *lose* weight? Yes. On average, women typically gain five pounds in their first trimester. But if you are not feeling well and even throwing up, it is not unheard of to lose weight in your first trimester. *Don't panic*—your healthcare provider will keep a close eye on your weight. If you're really worried about your baby's development, ask about the possibility of an ultrasound.

Also, don't be alarmed if, in the last month of pregnancy, you notice that you're not gaining as much as you had before—or maybe you've lost a little. Your baby is getting big, and there isn't as much amniotic fluid as there used to be.

Your Size and Others' Comments

Don't let other people's comments and opinions about your pregnancy drive you crazy! I used to be amused by the comments, but the ones about my size did bother me: "You can't possibly be six months pregnant! Where's the baby?" I used to get that a lot, and being a first-time mom, of course it caused me to worry.

Just keep in mind that every pregnant woman shows and gains weight differently. Also, as my doctor noted, "It's not how big your belly looks, it's how you measure lying down." After all the comments, I ended up with a baby in the ninety-seventh percentile for height and weight. As long as you and your healthcare provider are happy with the progress at each routine checkup, you're doing just fine.

Dealing with Your Burgeoning Belly

Will an Impact Hurt the Baby?

I did a few klutzy things during my pregnancy, all of which scared me to death. Two moments that really stand out are when I walked into an open car door and when I poked myself in the stomach while sweeping the kitchen floor. *Don't panic:* if you're OK, your baby is OK. In the beginning of your pregnancy, the pelvic bone is your baby's big protector. Once the baby gets bigger and your stomach grows over your pelvic bone, you still have built-in shock absorbers in your stomach muscles, and your uterus is also a big protective muscle. Let's not forget about the biggest protector of all: the amniotic fluid. It's like floating in a cloud!

The following is an extreme story and a reason why you shouldn't be riding a bike during your pregnancy. I tell it to you *only* to reassure you if you experienced a minor bump to the stomach, like I did. My friend Nancy was riding her bike while seven months pregnant, and she fell over the handlebars and skidded on her stomach! Sounds awful, doesn't it? But the baby was fine. Your bulging belly may seem more vulnerable than it really is.

How to Wear Seat Belts

Buckle up—even when you're nine months pregnant! Just be sure to keep the lap belt directly over your pelvis bone, under your protruding belly and not across it. The shoulder belt should rest comfortably between your breasts. Keeping yourself protected keeps your baby protected.

The First Fetal Movements

I made the mistake of reading a book that said at a certain month, you should feel a certain amount of fluttering or kicking movement. That did me in! Feeling your baby move gives you tremendous peace of mind, but keep in mind that every pregnancy is different. Most women feel movement at around nineteen to twenty-one weeks; others may not feel movement until twenty-two to twenty-four weeks with their first baby! (With your second baby, you may feel movement earlier—as early as fourteen to eighteen weeks.) Your baby's early movements may feel like twitches, gurgles, or bubbles; you may even mistake them for gas.

Fetal Movements Later in Pregnancy

A common concern for many women is the amount of fetal movement in the latter part of pregnancy. When you start to feel movement, around the fifth or sixth month, it's a wonderful assurance that everything's OK. You tend to rely on that constant reassurance that all is well with the baby. It's when you *don't* feel movement for periods of time that you begin to panic.

Babies sleep anywhere from thirty to sixty minutes at a time, and when you're walking and active during the day, you may be distracted from feeling movements. "Don't be concerned if you don't feel a lot of movement before the twenty-four-week point," says Jay Ugol, MD. Once you're at twenty-four weeks, here's what you can do to check movement: Eat or drink something with a little sugar, then lie down for an hour with no distractions. If you don't count at least ten movements within that hour, call your healthcare provider. He or she may recommend a fetal monitoring tracing, also called a non-stress test. Don't panic—most results come back perfectly normal.

Is Lying on Your Back OK?

If you've ever lain on your back during the latter part of your pregnancy, don't worry; you haven't harmed the baby. You may simply experience light-headedness and slight nausea because of a drop in blood pressure. "As the uterus grows up and out of your pelvis, it rests on the *vena cava* vein, which returns blood back to the heart," says Jay Ugol, MD. "Therefore, if you have less blood returning to your heart, you also have less blood pumping to all your organs, including the uterus." But the baby will be fine, so just relax and reposition yourself.

Dr. Ugol recommends sleeping on your left side during pregnancy. "If you tilt to the left side when lying down, the pressure of the growing uterus is lessened, and you have better blood flow for both you and your baby. You do not have to be *completely* on your left side; a pillow wedged under your right side will give you enough tilt to relieve the pressure. Don't feel paranoid or guilty if you wake in the middle of the night on your back; it's just good to get in the habit of sleeping to the left."

"I Don't Feel Pregnant!"

You've complained about morning sickness, the extreme fatigue, your tender breasts, and your irritability and then, all of a sudden, you don't feel pregnant and you want all those symptoms back! If this is happening to you, it's probably around the three-month mark and things are beginning to settle down. Your body has been busy. Your baby has grown all his major organs, the placenta has been growing and nesting into the lining of your womb, and your baby is now able to start functioning on his own and begin growing! It's a strange time for you, as you're feeling better yet still not showing. Not to worry. Soon enough, you will feel pregnant again . . . and very pregnant!

Changes in Your Digestion

Indigestion

That burning sensation is not a reason to be concerned, but it may drive you crazy! I was addicted to Tums; you don't have to worry about that either, for they're perfectly safe and a great source of calcium. (If Tums give you constipation, you can use liquid Mylanta or Maalox instead; it's less constipating and coats your esophagus as well as relieving indigestion.)

When your womb grows, it presses on your stomach, causing your stomach acids to overflow into your esophagus, which causes uncomfortable indigestion and heartburn. Here are a few things that may help.

Heartburn Helpers

- Try eating smaller meals throughout the day instead of three big meals.
- Sit up straight when eating.

- Avoid fried or spicy foods.
- Sleep propped up, using lots of pillows on your bed. This helps to keep stomach acid in your stomach and not in your throat.
- Drink plenty of milk, which soothes heartburn, and keep a glass nearby at night for midnight attacks.

Hemorrhoids

During pregnancy, your uterus and your growing baby rest on major blood vessels around the lower intestine. The extra pressure can cause them to bulge—a painful condition known as hemorrhoids. Hemorrhoids can be internal or external; don't be alarmed if you see a spot of fresh, red blood accompanied by pain and itching in your anal area. You may also experience hemorrhoids after delivery from the pressure of pushing out the baby.

How to Ease Hemorrhoids

- Keep your bowels moving and soft by eating extra fiber.
- If you do become constipated, don't strain to have a bowel movement. The straining causes extra pressure.
- Avoid sitting on hard surfaces.
- Soothe with warm sitz baths.
- If you're very sore, use an unscented baby wipe rather than toilet paper. Wipes containing witch hazel also soothe hemorrhoids.

Gas and Constipation

During pregnancy, your digestive system and your bowel movements slow down, creating a great environment for gas and constipation. (Lucky you!) The good news is, they're certainly not going to hurt your baby, and there are some ways to avoid the discomfort.

Gas pains are probably the most uncomfortable pains imaginable. I didn't have this problem in my first pregnancy, but early on in my second pregnancy, every night I was plagued with it. If you have fingerlike pains surrounding your stomach, with a sense of fullness and pressure, it's gas. If it feels more like menstrual cramping and you have other symptoms, such as bleeding or nausea, you should contact your doctor.

You can help fight off gas by exercising, not gulping your drinks, and avoiding carbonated drinks. A fiber-rich diet can also help. Leafy greens, other vegetables, and bran are all good sources of fiber, and many foods are now labeled "high-fiber." Peppermint tea can help, too. If you are really suffering, see page 31 for a safe over-the-counter gas medication.

Constipation is easier to pinpoint than gas but no less annoying. And it can lead to hemorrhoids. You can help yourself stay "regular" by increasing your fiber and water intake.

Stretch Marks

If your mother had stretch marks, chances are, you will have them, too. These white, pinkish, or red lines have nothing to do with how much weight you gain; heredity plays a big role. The good news is that they'll fade over time and become less noticeable. Keep sunscreen on your stretch marks when you're out in the sun, so they won't stand out from the surrounding skin.

"Why Is My Skin Getting Darker?"

Toward the end of pregnancy, many women notice the sudden appearance of a mysterious, dark, vertical line down the middle of the belly. It's called *linea nigra*—Latin for "dark line"—and it's caused by skin pigmentation where your abdominal muscles have stretched to accommodate your growing baby. The darker your skin tone, the darker the line is apt to be. But don't worry—it will disappear completely after pregnancy.

You may also notice other areas on your body turning darker, such as your nipples, moles, and freckles. This is called the *mask of pregnancy*. A few months after delivery, these darker patches and the line on your stomach will fade.

Bladder Control

If a sneeze or cough causes you to leak a little urine, it's because your growing baby is placing pressure on your bladder. (It's unlikely that this leakage is your water breaking, but if you have any questions, call your healthcare provider.)

You may notice that you have this tremendous need to go to the bathroom only to find out that you don't have to go. Try rocking back and forth on the toilet: this lessens the pressure of the womb on the bladder so that you release the flow of urine.

Swelling and Water Retention

When I was seven months pregnant and out to dinner with friends, I looked down to find that my ankles had swelled to double their size! I didn't know whether to laugh or cry.

Beth Iovinelli reassured me: "During pregnancy, swelling of the ankles, feet, and hands is normal—and quite common. The medical name for this is *dependent edema,* which means swelling that's dependent on gravity. It happens when your body holds on to water, and this accounts for some of that weight you have been gaining! It's not harmful; just put your feet up."

If you notice swelling in other parts of your body, such as your face, you may have *nondependent edema* (swelling that's not related to gravity), which could indicate preeclampsia. Call your healthcare provider.

Ways to Reduce Swelling

- Elevate your feet when possible. Keep a stool or pile of books under your desk; at home, lie on your left side when possible.
- If you're really desperate, put on waist-high support tights before you get out of bed in the morning, so that fluid has no chance to pool around your ankles.
- Drink plenty of water. Surprisingly, keeping hydrated helps your body retain less water.
- Exercise regularly—especially by walking, swimming, or riding an exercise bike.
- Avoid sodium and salty foods such as olives and salted nuts.

Nosebleeds

You may never have had a nosebleed before in your life, but as the volume of blood in your pregnant body increases, you may find yourself suffering from them frequently. To avoid this annoying problem, keep your nasal passages moist with a little Vaseline, a humidifier, or a water mister designed for dry noses. If a nosebleed does occur, pinch your nose closed for at least ten minutes and—contrary to what you may think— tip your head *forward,* not backward. (If you tip it backward, the blood will just run down your throat.) One more tip: once you've stopped the bleeding, try not to blow your nose for a while!

Bleeding, Irritated Gums

Bleeding gums are another annoyance of pregnancy. I checked with Michael N. Pomarico, DMD, a dentist in Norwalk, Connecticut, to make sure bleeding gums were normal. "It has been my experience in the past thirty-five years that a large percentage of women experience some changes in their oral health during pregnancy," he says. "There are many hormonal changes that take place, and this may lead to swelling and bleeding of the gums due to engorgement of the blood in that area."

What to do? Keep up with your normal routine of brushing and flossing, but gently.

If the thought of a toothbrush coming in contact with your mouth causes you to gag because of morning sickness, try mouthwashes with anti-plaque and fluoride solutions until the gag reflex passes.

Shortness of Breath

Don't be surprised when a short walk makes you short of breath. Granted, it was a hot, 90°F summer day and I was eight months pregnant when it happened to me. But it still was shocking. After all, I felt I was in good shape. I had even been walking two miles a day. So, why the shortness of breath? The baby is getting larger and taking up more room, which means your lungs have less room to expand. But even though you may be huffing and puffing, rest assured that your baby is getting plenty of oxygen. Your lungs actually expand during pregnancy, and you breathe a bit faster and deeper. You may also find yourself yawning more often. These are all your body's ways of boosting the baby's oxygen supply.

In addition to yawning, you may notice that you can't catch a full breath, yet you're not breathing any faster than usual. This is called *air hunger,* and it's nothing to worry about. It's caused by elevated progesterone levels and by your growing baby pushing on your diaphragm.

On the other hand, if you have rapid shallow breathing, it's time to call your healthcare provider. This phenomenon is called *tachypnea,* and you should be seen immediately.

Leg Cramps

You may notice leg cramping—again, not a reason to panic. It's just hard to leap from the bed in pain from a charley horse when you're eight months pregnant. It's best to stand up and put your weight on that leg, or stretch the toes upward toward your knee.

Round Ligament Pain

The large stomach muscles that support your pelvis and your growing belly are called round ligament muscles. As your belly expands, these muscles stretch to accommodate the baby. The stretching can cause mild aches and pains, especially after a long day. You may notice this slight pain around the second trimester. Look at your stomach—it's stretching!

Braxton-Hicks Contractions

Toward the end of pregnancy, it's not uncommon to feel occasional cramping in your uterus that lasts for about a minute. *Don't panic*—it's not labor! It's just Braxton-Hicks contractions: your uterine muscles tightening and contracting to prepare your body for childbirth. True labor pains come with regularity, whereas Braxton-Hicks are rather sporadic. This may sound annoying, but you'll know when it's the real thing! (If you are really unsure, just check with your healthcare provider.)

LET'S GO SHOPPING! WHAT YOU NEED, WHAT YOU DON'T, AND WHERE TO PUT IT

Don't Panic over Baby Supplies

Shopping for your baby is one of the most exciting and emotionally fraught parts of pregnancy. It's easy to get obsessed with creating the perfect nursery. But take it from someone who knows: there's no need to feel overwhelmed. Moms and babies have managed with minimal supplies for more than 100,000 years.

Choosing the Right Car Seat

The primary consideration when buying a car seat is, of course, safety. Newborns need a rear-facing car seat, and it should be installed in the back seat of your car. It must be secured snugly, without rocking from side to side or slipping from front to back, or it's not going to protect your baby.

The best way to ensure a proper installation is to attend a car-seat safety check before your baby arrives. (See also page 131.) Many police and fire departments and hospitals offer periodic safety check meetings. If you can't find a meeting near you, call your local police department: sometimes, a particular officer on the force handles car-seat checks by appointment.

I recommend buying the type of infant car seat that can detach from its base. You keep the base in the car and carry the seat with you, with the baby strapped in. You can buy an extra base for a second car. "Travel systems" are also available, with a car seat that fits into a stroller. With car seats that travel with you, you never have to wake a sleeping baby!

A Place for Your Baby to Sleep

Many experienced moms will tell you that wherever your baby will sleep best is the best place for your baby to be. That may be in a separate room in a crib, in a bassinet for the first couple of months, or right next to you, snuggled into a family bed (see the tips starting on page 102). I even know one baby who slept best in his car seat!

Do what feels right for you and your baby. If it feels right and everyone is getting some sleep, then that's all that matters. And remember, nothing is a constant with babies. Their sleeping preferences may change overnight, so be flexible!

Educating Yourself about SIDS

The thought of sudden infant death syndrome, or SIDS, is terrifying to parents of a newborn. SIDS affects children under the age of one year, and in most cases, it occurs within the first six months of life. It's also known as *crib death,* since most SIDS deaths occur at night. Children with SIDS simply stop breathing and die, for reasons that are still uncertain.

The most important thing you can do to help prevent SIDS is to always put your child to sleep on her back, on a firm, certified baby mattress. The crib should be as sparse as possible, so that your child can't bury her face in a blanket, pillow, puffy bumper pads, or a stuffed animal. If you have a cute quilt or pillow in your child's crib for decoration, remove it when you put your baby in! For added peace of mind, you can purchase a "sleeping wedge," which has two sides to prevent your baby from rolling over.

Please speak with your healthcare provider for more detailed information about SIDS. You can also contact the SIDS Alliance by calling (800) 221-7437, or on the Web at www.sidsalliance.org.

Is Co-Sleeping Safe?

Yes, done properly, co-sleeping is safe. It can be a wonderful experience for you *and* your baby as long as you do it responsibly (see the following tips). It's especially nice for working moms: you get an extra eight hours of bonding and cuddling! Co-sleeping makes nighttime breastfeeding easier, and the comfort of having you near can help your baby sleep more soundly. That, in turn, means extra precious sleep for you.

You'll know when it's the right time to introduce your child to her crib. Don't put any needless time constraints on yourself. If you and your baby are happy with your sleeping arrangements, then don't worry about other people's comments.

Some Tips for Co-Sleeping

- Make sure you have a firm mattress (not a water- or featherbed) with plenty of room for an extra person. Push your mattress against the wall, and wedge a tightly rolled-up blanket snugly into the space between mattress and wall, so there is no gap. Have your baby sleep next to the wall.

- Mom should sleep next to the baby, on the opposite side from the wall. Mothers seem to have "antennae" for sensing the whereabouts of a baby in bed with them, so they're less likely to roll over on a baby during sleep. Dads often develop this sense over time, but little kids just don't have it. Don't let other children sleep next to your baby.

- Put your baby to sleep on her back, just as in a crib. To avoid overheating, use only light covers and light clothing on your baby. Your body heat will help to keep her warm.

- Don't co-sleep under the influence of alcohol or any drowsiness-inducing drug. And don't co-sleep if you're feeling so sleep-deprived that you think you'll sleep like a log. Also, if you're very overweight, it's best not to co-sleep; you're at risk for sleep apnea, which can compromise your awareness of your baby.

- If you're nervous about co-sleeping, buy a co-sleeping bassinet that at-taches to your bed but gives your baby her own safe space.

- For more in-depth information on co-sleeping, look for books by Dr. William Sears. He is probably the best-known advocate for co-sleeping.

Choosing a Crib

When purchasing a crib, what are you looking for? You're probably looking for a certain style that suits your nursery, and there are many to choose from. But the most important thing is the mattress.

When choosing our crib, I was told to put our money in the mattress and not in the crib. The baby doesn't care about what her crib looks like; she wants a good, firm mattress! Mattresses also come with two degrees of firmness: a rock-hard side for the baby's first year, and a softer side for when he's a year old. Just flip the mattress when the baby is ready.

Really Useful Items

Beyond a car seat and a place for the baby to sleep, you really only need a few supplies during those first precious weeks:

- Newborn diapers
- Baby wipes. I found that the generic pharmacy wipes are the best, because they are thin and very moist.
- Diaper rash ointment. The generic brand works just as well as the others.
- A digital thermometer. Make sure you know how to use it before you need it.
- A soft emery board or an infant nail clipper
- Cotton balls and rubbing alcohol to dry the umbilical cord in those first couple of weeks, until it falls off
- At least ten thin, cotton washcloths
- Cetaphil or other mild soap for shampooing and washing the baby's skin (available at pharmacies and some larger supermarkets)
- A soft toothbrush to comb the baby's fine hair. The bristles are extra soft on your baby's scalp. Or you can buy a baby brush—not because the baby really needs it, but because it's fun to use!

- A cheap, hard-bristled brush is great for brushing away cradle cap. (See page 165.)
- At least ten receiving blankets
- At least six layette gowns with open, elasticized bottoms (instead of snaps) for quick diaper changes in the middle of the night
- A plastic baby bathtub
- Bottles and nipples, if you plan to use a bottle (see page 214–20)
- Ten burp cloths. Plain cloth diapers are inexpensive and they work just fine.
- A baby monitor. If you receive two sets at a baby shower, keep both—you'll use them!

Goodies You Can Live Without

Like many new moms, I bought a Diaper Genie, and it was so complicated that I had to have a friend come over to help me install the bags that create the little "sausage link" casings for the baby's poops. When it came time to replace the bags, just a day or two later, I was in tears. Over-tired and a bit overwhelmed, I just couldn't deal with the frustration of not being able to figure out how to install them. The solution? I never used it again and have never once missed it! I use a regular wastepaper basket with a lid and keep the plastic liners at the bottom for quick refills. When your baby begins to crawl, make sure to remove the plastic liners, as they pose a suffocation hazard.

You may be under the assumption that baby clothes require baby detergent. I have to admit, it was fun after my baby shower to get the nurs-ery ready by washing all the baby's clothes in a special detergent. It smells so good! But don't feel compelled to buy that expensive baby deter-gent; a mild, perfume-free detergent is just as good for your baby as it is for your clothes.

Beth Iovinelli adds, "Most baby product manufacturers make new parents think they need to break the bank in order to be prepared. Keep it simple! If it seems frivolous or unnecessary, it probably is."

Getting the Most from Your Gift Registry

When registering for your baby's gifts, keep in mind that she won't need a lot of toys in her first couple of months. These are a few things that I found very helpful:

- A soft, vibrating baby sling/chair
- A feeding pillow (such as a Boppy) to help support the baby during feedings
- A vibrating swing
- Just a few small toys and rattles to stimulate her. At this age, Mom's face, Dad's tie, shadows on the wall, a light, a ceiling fan, or looking out

the window is enough to keep your baby entertained.

- A baby sling to keep her close to you and content, as you do errands around the house or take a walk outside for fresh air.

As babies get older and are able to support their heads (around three months), they'll enjoy these toys:

- A bouncy seat that you install in a door jamb
- A "tummy time" toy. It's a toy that encourages your baby to hold her head up when she is placed on her stomach.
- An entertainment saucer. It's a large, round plastic toy (no wheels!) that has a soft, bouncy seat in the center. The baby can spin, jump, and play; and you can get things done around the house or—better yet—relax for ten minutes!

It's a good idea to register for toys that your baby will enjoy throughout her entire first year. Store the toys and equipment in the basement or attic. Then, when you notice that your baby is moving on to the next stage, you'll be prepared. Instead of making a shopping expedition, you can just take a quick trip to the basement.

Keeping Track of Weight Limits

Many toys and pieces of baby equipment have guidelines for age and weight. Use a label maker or a permanent marker and write all the important information directly on the car seat, stroller, bouncy seat, etc. That way, when the second baby comes along or you give your old baby equipment to a friend, you'll feel reassured knowing that all the pertinent information is right at your fingertips.

Assemble Your Purchases Beforehand

Before our baby arrived, my husband and I spent many nights on the kitchen floor with instruction manuals and little plastic parts scattered throughout the kitchen. Beware: most baby equipment needs to be assembled! I recommend doing it before the baby arrives. It's also a good idea to know how to use your new equipment beforehand. The last thing you want is to be fighting with the stroller in a rainy parking lot with a crying baby.

Start a Filing System

Keep instruction manuals and warranty cards around in case of recalls or lost parts. Before the baby arrives, get a filing box to hold your baby-related paperwork. In addition, you can file doctors' records, birth certificates, Social Security cards, child care information, and maternity leave paperwork.

Setting Up the Nursery

Small nurseries are cozy and inviting. Here are some space-saving tips that work well. After all, a baby doesn't need a lot of space. All he needs is you!

A Soothing Light Source

When it's 3:00 A.M., the baby is hungry, and you're half-asleep, the last thing you want is a harsh light on in the nursery. Keep a night light near your rocking chair or bedside table if you like to nurse in bed. You can also install a dimmer switch in your bedroom and in the nursery.

Extra Shelves

One way to combat a small space is to use plenty of shelves. Get things up and off the ground! For extra ointments, burp cloths, diapers, and other things for the changing table, put up shelves or mount bins on the wall close to your changing area—but never directly above it.

It's best to keep these items up and away because by six months of age, your baby will be using them as toys at changing time!

How to Make a Closet Armoire

If your nursery is small, like mine is, and there really is no extra room for a dresser, use the closet to its fullest. My son's hanging clothes are not very long, so we installed two shelves just below the hanging area and one shelf just above the closet rod. Everything he needs fits perfectly in the closet—and if it gets a little messy, I just shut the door.

A Hanging Shoe Organizer

When we were turning our guest bedroom into the nursery, I kept the shoe organizer on the closet door. It has twenty-four sections that were just the right size for all the little extras: a pocket for socks, washcloths, hats, baby CDs, creams, first-aid supplies, and other odds and ends. It really helps to keep things organized, and if you buy one with clear plastic pockets, you can easily see what's inside.

The Power of Plastic Bins

Prepare now for your future storage needs! In the blink of an eye, your baby will go from being seven pounds to twenty pounds—and with it will go a lot of clothes. Buy clear plastic bins with lids for future storage, and pre-label them by size, type, and season. (Always keep a bin in the closet: when clothes are too small, you can reorganize in a flash.)

Keeping Clothes Organized

- Baby clothes are so tiny that they can be hard to fold and hard to keep organized in big spaces. To alleviate this problem, buy compartmental shelving for the drawers in your dresser.

- Baby clothes typically run 0–3 months, 3–6 months, 6–9 months, 9–12, 12–18, etc. To keep the different sizes organized, you can section off the closet rod with tags or ribbons to indicate the next size up.
- Keep bigger sizes of clothes on hand; you won't believe how soon you'll need them!

PREPARING FOR THE BIG DAY: A LITTLE ORGANIZATION GOES A LONG WAY

Preparing Yourself Mentally

Take a Childbirth Class!

"Childbirth classes, no matter what school of thought you choose, have two main purposes," says Jay Ugol, MD. "One is to know your options—for instance, you may not want an epidural, but it's best to know your options for pain relief. The second is to take the fear out of the unknown."

Childbirth classes help you prepare for the surprises that can happen during labor and delivery, and they help your husband or partner become more involved in the birthing process. Breathing techniques are also a big part of most classes; they can significantly reduce your pain and panic during labor and delivery.

Rhythmic Breathing

Don't panic if you can't remember all the breathing techniques they teach you in childbirth class—you're not alone. The one technique that I was able to master is called "ocean breath." Slowly and deeply breathe in through your nose, and slowly exhale. Continue to take slow, deep breaths, but slightly contract the back of your throat. You should hear a quiet hissing sound, like the ocean (actually, I always think of Darth Vader in *Star Wars*). It's good to practice daily.

If You Are Having a C-Section

More and more women are giving birth by cesarean section. The national average for C-sections is now 20 to 25 percent of all births. If you're a candidate for a C-section, there's no need to panic!

"In general, C-sections are relatively safe procedures when performed by a board-certified OB/GYN and anesthesiologist," says Jay Ugol, MD. "Make sure you've discussed the risks and benefits of all of your options with your healthcare provider, and that you understand and agree as to why you're having a C-section." It's worth getting the information even if you don't anticipate needing a C-section. If your labor isn't progressing and your provider decides a C-section is necessary, you'll know what to expect—and not to panic!

The average C-section takes less than sixty minutes. The recovery is longer than for vaginal deliveries. You'll typically have a four-day hospital stay for a cesarean birth, compared with a two-day stay for a vaginal birth.

To learn more about C-sections, look for *The Essential C-Section Guide* by Maureen Connolly and Dana Sullivan (Broadway Books, 2004).

Coping with Your Fear of Pain

I didn't really begin to obsess on the pain of childbirth until my ninth month. But when I just couldn't believe my belly was going to get any bigger, I started to panic: how was I physically going to get the baby out?

My solution was to have an epidural, ASAP! My water broke on Friday night and my son wasn't born until Sunday night. I had one night of intense, period-like pains at home; but when I arrived at the hospital, they gave me my epidural, so the rest of labor wasn't all that painful.

Whether or not to have an epidural is a very personal decision. Many women manage their pain without one, by using breathing techniques, visualization, and/or a variety of birthing positions. But even if you're planning for an all-natural childbirth, it's best to learn about epidurals beforehand, just in case. Your childbirth class, your healthcare provider, or an anesthesiologist can give you a detailed overview.

"All hospitals should follow a strict protocol with an epidural, administered by a board-certified anesthesiologist," says Jay Ugol, MD. "It's a relatively safe procedure, and serious complications are rare. Spinal headaches from the epidural shot are unlikely but can occur and they're very treatable once recognized."

It's also not as hard as you might think to sit still while they put the needle in. It feels like a minor bee sting while it's happening, and after a night of labor, that feels pretty good! After delivery, the most common complaint about epidurals is a sore spot or bruised feeling where the needle was inserted.

Make a Birthing Plan

There are many different pain-relief alternatives and delivery styles to choose from. Discuss them all with your partner and healthcare provider, and have a general plan that you're comfortable with. But don't put unnecessary pressure on yourself if your dream delivery doesn't go as scripted: nature has a way of foiling the best-laid plans!

"Will I Have a BM on the Delivery Table?"

Many delivery nurses will tell you to push as if you are having a bowel movement. Will you actually have one—right there on the table in front of everyone? It's a common worry. But trust me: though you may be cringing now, during delivery you just won't care. Nothing is held back during birth—it's a very primal experience. You probably won't even know whether you had a bowel movement, and your husband will never tell!

Preparing Yourself Physically

The Value of a Little Exercise

It really helps if you're in good physical shape before delivering a baby. I didn't fully realize this before getting pregnant, but after pushing for three hours, I had a better understanding of what "being in shape" means. When your ankles are wrapped around your head in the delivery room, you, too, will have a better understanding of what I'm talking about.

As for me, I was so sore the next day, I could hardly get out of bed. And it wasn't just from the obvious pain of delivering a baby: it was my muscles. I felt as if I'd just run three marathons! I wasn't too surprised to learn later that the energy needed to run a marathon is comparable to the energy needed for labor. No wonder I felt so bad . . . I didn't have that energy!

Getting in Shape for Labor

Don't panic if you're not in terrific shape already, because it's never too late to improve your fitness. Just be sure to check first with your health-care provider. Even if you're in your ninth month, you can usually go for a walk, lift light weights, and try to do some light stretching. Swimming is another great low-impact exercise—plus, it makes you feel much more buoyant (a welcome sensation in the last trimester, believe me).

How Will Your Water Break?

Lots of late-term pregnant women worry that their water will break suddenly and forcefully in a public place. Only 30 percent, or roughly one-third, of women experience their water breaking before they go into labor. (See page 126 for tips if you're really concerned about this.)

Most women whose water has broken will be contracting on their own within twenty-four hours. If your water hasn't broken, your health-care provider may break it for you at the hospital, using an Amni-Hook, a crochet-needle-shaped device. This process is called *artificial rupture of membranes*. Although the Amni-Hook looks fierce, it won't hurt the baby at all. You may experience slight discomfort and cramping when your water is being broken.

When the water breaks, the fluid won't nec-essarily come gushing out all at once. The baby's head may act like a cork, and you very well may have a slow trickle. Contact your doctor immedi-ately if your water breaks before you're at the hospital; most obstetricians recommend delivery within twenty-four to forty-eight hours to prevent infection. If it's the middle of the night, your healthcare provider will probably ask you a few questions: Can you feel the baby moving? Is the amniotic fluid clear? (If the fluid is greenish or brownish, it could indicate the presence of meconium—your baby's first stool—and your provider will bring you in for a non-stress test, to check on the baby.) Next, your provider will check your records to make sure you are not a carrier of group B strep.

Your healthcare provider will decide how to proceed based on the results of your group B strep test, the presence or absence of meconium, the ripeness of your cervix, and feedback from a fetal and contraction monitor.

Stock Up on Sanitary Napkins

You may not have used these in a really long time, but soon they'll be indispensable! You may need them if your water breaks at home, and you'll need them for two to six weeks after delivery, while your body is still recovering from childbirth.

Amniotic Fluid: Go with the Flow

Breaking water, even in public, is perfectly natural. Don't worry about it. (After all, your child will provide plenty of embarrassment in the years to come: exploding poopy diapers, projectile spitup, temper tantrums . . . the list goes on.) However, if you'd rather play it safe, here are a few helpful hints.

- If you're really terrified of your water breaking in public, wear an "adult undergarment" such as Depend.
- Keep towels in your car for emergencies and to sit on while in transit.
- If you're worried about your water breaking while you're asleep, put a shower curtain liner under your bottom sheet.
- If you think your water has broken, call your healthcare provider.

When to Call Your Healthcare Provider

During late pregnancy especially, you have enough on your mind without suffering your fears in silence. Call your healthcare provider when you are the slightest bit concerned: that's what she's there for! And you should definitely call if:

- you're having contractions every five minutes (for your first baby) or every five to ten minutes (for subsequent babies);
- you're leaking amniotic fluid, not mucus;
- you notice decreased fetal movement; or
- you have bleeding.

When to Go to the Hospital

You may have read a lot of different opinions as to when you should actually go to the hospital. Talk with your healthcare provider and make a plan that you feel good about. My doctor wanted me to feel comfortable and safe, so he advised me to go when I personally felt ready. *There is nothing wrong with being sent home!*

My water broke at midnight on Friday, and my doctor wanted to meet me at the hospital the next morning at 6:00 A.M. regardless of how far apart my contractions were. We met and updated the game plan, then I went home. *I was not ashamed;* I took one look at the delivery room and wanted to get out of there! The next morning, I went back to the same delivery room, and this time I was ready to stay.

Keep the Tank Full

Avoid a real panic by keeping the car gassed up at all times during your third trimester! You don't want your gas gauge to read empty when you're rushing to the hospital.

What to Pack

Packing for the hospital is really a personal thing. By all means, bring whatever makes you feel comfortable and happy. Here are a few things I couldn't have done without:

- An outfit to wear home. You'll be leaving a little smaller—but not that small. Think of yourself at five months pregnant.
- Comfortable clothes to wear while you're there. *Do not* run out and buy the perfect pajamas and a beautiful robe to lounge around the hospital in. There are still quite a number of fluids pouring from your body, and you won't want to ruin anything special.
- All the toiletries and makeup that make you feel good! It's nice to take a hot shower, wash your hair, and put on a nice moisturizer and lip balm.

- A folder for all the documents you'll receive and have to sign. Some hospitals will provide this, but an extra one never hurts.
- And don't forget your phone list of people to call once the baby arrives!

Bring an Extra Bag

You'll be amazed at the amount of stuff you accumulate at the hospital. To avoid rummaging through the maternity maintenance room—as my husband did, looking for an empty box—take along an extra bag and a box for bringing flowers home.

Getting the Car Seat Ready

Car seats caused me to *panic*. You can avoid that by having a professional install the car seat. Check with your local police department, fire station, or car dealership, or with the store where you bought the seat. Sometimes, they offer car-seat installation programs.

Install the car seat at least a month before the baby's due date, just in case he arrives early. And learn how to use the seat before the baby arrives. If I had it to do over again, I'd practice first with a doll or a teddy bear. When it came time for my husband to check us out of the hospital, he brought the car seat into my hospital room and placed my fragile baby in the seat. I took one look and realized that I had absolutely no idea how to buckle him in! A nurse had to come in and do it for us, which I'm sure she'd done many times before.

Take a CPR Class

It's a great idea to attend a CPR and basic first-aid class with your husband or partner before the baby arrives. Believe it or not, in no time, your baby will be eating solid foods and you won't have an extra minute to attend a several-hour CPR class. Check with your local Red Cross for class information; the courses generally cover breathing, cardiac emergencies, and sudden illness and injuries. It's a wise time investment. You won't panic every time there's a slight gurgle or a gag when you're feeding your baby, and you'll rest assured that you can take care of bumps and bruises.

AT THE HOSPITAL: POINTERS FOR THE PROUDEST (AND MOST CONFUSING) MOMENTS OF YOUR LIFE

Make Yourself at Home

Once you're settled into your hospital room, take a little time to learn your way around the floor. Get to know your nurse: share any concerns or fears you have, and tell her about your hopes for the birthing process. Find out where the ice machine is for ice chips to suck on, and find out where your partner can get warm blankets if you're feeling chilled. Don't be shy about walking around and saying hello—you'll have a much better hospital experience that way.

Don't Push with Your Face

No one told me not to push with my face! Had that been the only thing I learned at Lamaze, the class would have been worthwhile. After three hours of pushing, my eyes were so swollen shut that when the baby *finally* arrived, I had to squint to see him—otherwise, I saw three babies. I don't know who looked worse, the baby or me. With the harsh lights of the delivery room, he was squinting his swollen eyes up at me and I was squinting back at him, and we looked like we were both from the same planet waiting for the mother ship to take us home. But there was no mistaking, the two of us belonged together.

To avoid looking like I did, when it's time to push, push like you're having a bowel movement. You can also practice pushing beforehand from your stomach: curl your pelvis in a C shape, and get to know the muscles in your lower abdomen and not in your eyes. Kegel exercises can also help (see page 65).

Cold Packs for Your Face

When I was recovering from delivery, the nurses at the hospital gave me some high-tech sanitary napkins that become chilled when you twist them. They're meant for your underwear (and you'll know why!), but I set one aside to soothe my puffy eyes. Ask if you can take a couple home with you.

"My Baby Is Funny-Looking!"

Everyone is cooing and gushing over your beautiful Gerber baby, and you think, *Wow! I really created a beautiful baby!* You anxiously await the handover of your beautiful creation . . . and then you gasp! *That is no Gerber baby!* After three hours of pushing, your baby came out with a cone head, swollen eyes, and an ear curled over. You're too embarrassed to ask, but you're wondering: Will it all go away? Even the hairy back?

The reason Gerber babies are so perfect-looking is that they're not actually newborns! Newborns do not always look like china dolls, unless you've had a C-section, which is a little easier on the baby. The birthing process is tough on babies, but they're built to handle it. I pushed for three hours with my son, and he came out with a cone-shaped head and an elongated forehead from "molding" (his skull bones literally molded to fit through the birth canal). By the time he left the hospital, though, he had a nice round head.

Your baby's eyes will be puffy from water retention, and he'll certainly be squinting in the bright light. His eyes may even be blood-shot from the pressure of delivery. His face may appear misshapen, with a flattened nose, from the tight squeeze through the birth canal.

The fine, peach-fuzz hair from his back to his earlobes is called lanugo. That, too, will disappear. He may also have blotchy skin, with some areas ranging from pink to purple. This is from his immature circulatory system, which is just getting used to life outside the womb.

Don't feel uncomfortable about asking a nurse about your baby's appearance, and rest assured: all these little oddities will disappear within days.

Your Body's Self-Cleaning Process

After delivery, your body continues its self-cleaning process by discharging *lochia,* a bloody flow that gradually diminishes as your uterus returns to normal. You can expect heavy, period-type blood for the first couple of days; it may contain blood clots. Within the first week, the blood should turn from a bright red to brown. The entire flow of lochia can last for two to six weeks.

Don't panic if you also discharge some water. This is not at all common, but it happened to me. The day after I delivered, I was lying in bed when all of a sudden, I released a pool of water. Think about all that water you retain during pregnancy; this was how my body got rid of some!

Night sweats are a much more common way for your body to eliminate excess water. Don't be surprised if you have them in the first couple of days postpartum.

Blood Clots Are Normal

It's common to pass a few blood clots after delivery, even when you're back at home. And you may experience slight cramping as your uterus expels them. "Blood has a natural tendency to clump and stick—a process called coagulation," says Beth Iovinelli. "This leads to clumps, or clots, of blood as your uterine lining is shed." Call your healthcare provider if you are soaking more than one sanitary pad an hour, if you're passing blood clots all the time, or if you notice that the clots are increasing in size. It's probably nothing serious, but it's always best to double-check.

Breastfeeding in the Delivery Room

No time like the present to start breastfeeding! You're in the delivery room for at least an hour after the baby is born, while the doctors are doing a little housekeeping (delivering the placenta, stitching you up if you had an episiotomy, and removing any number of tubes from your body). This downtime is a great opportunity to establish the breastfeeding process. Beth Iovinelli recommends asking a nurse to help you with your first breastfeeding experience.

Above all, be patient with yourself. Breastfeeding is a new skill, and it takes time to master for both you and your new baby!

The Benefits of Delivery-Room Breastfeeding

- You'll keep your baby warm with skin-to-skin contact.
- The colostrum (your high-protein, antibody-rich pre-milk) smells like amniotic fluid, which is comforting to your baby and helps attract him to your breast. And when he drinks it, it increases his blood glucose levels.
- The sucking will help to contract your uterus and control your bleeding.
- Many moms are apprehensive about being able to breastfeed, and the immediate experience increases their confidence right away.
- Last but not least, it feels great to finally hold your baby!

Thanks to Beth Iovinelli for this list.

Making the Most of Your Hospital Stay

After delivery, you may be exhausted, emotionally drained, and ready to sleep for three days straight. Not only would you like some time to recover from the strain of pregnancy at this point, but how does a spa package for a week to recoup from childbirth sound?

Sorry, that's probably not in your near future! So what's the next best thing? Sleep, rest, and restore as best you can in between feedings. And learn as much as you can from your nurses: they're your own personal baby- and self-care mentors for the next few days.

I wish I had managed my valuable time in the hospital better. Here are a few tips to help you recover:

- Take the phone off the hook when you're resting.

- If you have a large family, ask some or all of them to come to your home instead of to the hospital. I never thought I would say that—I was so excited to have tons of visitors—but when you have two groups of well-wishers show up at the same time and they don't know each other, with all of the necessary introductions you begin to feel as if you're entertaining.
- Enlist the nurses to help shield you from unnecessary intrusions by placing a sign on the door that says "Resting. Please come back later."

Beth Iovinelli puts it this way: "Think of the oxygen mask in a plane. They always tell you to put your mask on first, and then assist your child, which makes sense. How can you help your child if you've passed out from a lack of oxygen?" It's the same principle here: you need to take care of yourself in order to properly take care of your infant.

COMING HOME: SELF-CARE FOR SHELL-SHOCKED PARENTS

Getting Support for the "Fourth Trimester"

So, you just gave birth to your baby, and your pregnancy hormone ride is over . . . right? Not just yet. You still have to conquer the fourth trimester: the first three months that you are home with your baby. There's a good chance that you'll feel overwhelmed as you're trying to keep up with the needs of an infant—twenty-four hours a day, seven days a week—on very little sleep.

To help cope with this tremendous stress, a new mom needs support from her husband or partner, family, and friends. My son, Jimmy, was one week old when I went to my first support group for new moms. It took me about an hour to get out of the house, twenty minutes to drive to the hospital, and another twenty minutes to get from the parking lot to the room where the class was being held. When I finally settled in and looked around at the other women, who were equally tired and disheveled—all holding, feeding, changing, burping, and soothing their babies—I felt right at home. For the first time since leaving the hospital, I felt safe, and I was able to relax just knowing there were professionals all around us. Those wonderful maternity nurses who came running with the click of the call button during my stay at the hospital were, once again, right down the hall!

If you are able, do make the effort to attend the weekly support groups offered by hospitals and pediatricians' offices. You'll be really glad you did.

Avoid Long To-Do Lists

Rule #1 after bringing your baby home: *Don't cre-ate a long list of things that need attention in your house or apartment. It will induce panic.* If you make a list, keep it short. You'll find that it's hard just to get your teeth brushed some days, not to mention cleaning, cooking, and the host of other tasks you used to accomplish so easily!

Now is the time to let things go around the house and focus on your baby. And it's also the time to ask for help. If a friend is coming over for a visit, ask her to pick up some groceries or make a trip to the pharmacy for you. If Grandma is com-ing over, ask her to fold a load of laundry during her visit. *Don't be shy about asking for help.*

Be Realistic about Baby Calendars

Keeping a baby calendar can be a wonderfully rewarding exercise. How else can you remem-ber your baby's amazing progress? Don't feel pressure to create a new entry every single day, but do take time to write a quick note to record the milestones every so often.

Keeping Up with Thank-You Notes

It's amazing how many people think of you and your new baby by sending special gifts or cards. I tried to get my thank-you notes out as soon as I received a gift; it seems the longer you wait, the harder it is to get them done. Also, if you send the note right away, it can be short and to-the-point ("Thanks for the thoughtful gift for Jimmy. It was so nice of you to stop by . . ."). As a rule, the longer you wait, the longer the note should be—as you'll need to go into a little more detail about your new life with the baby.

To avoid a backlog of thank-you notes, it helps to be organized. Have your stationery and stamps on hand, so as soon as the gift arrives, you can send the note immediately.

Bad Hair Days

After my baby was born, I decided to go back to a short haircut. It was a messy bedhead-type cut and it had always looked good, even when I didn't wash it for a day or two. My beauty regimen was curtailed with a newborn, so what better time for a short, low-maintenance haircut?

Of course, when I cut my hair *this* time, it wasn't quite right. I even went back for a redo, but something had gone terribly wrong. My hair was not cooperating. Could it be those pregnancy hormones at work again, this time wreaking havoc on my hair? You bet! My hair had temporarily lost its old body and texture, a common experience for new moms.

To make matters worse, super-fine tufts of new hair started to grow around my hairline, giving me one-inch bangs, and they came in gray to boot! But wait. I then received another bonus: two tiny bald spots appeared—one on each side of my head near my temples!

The good news is that, for the first time in your life, you just won't care about your appearance all that much. You have a beautiful baby, and that puts things (such as how your hair looks) into proper perspective. In time, the texture will come back, the bangs will grow in . . . and a little color will take care of the gray.

Hair Loss

Around twelve weeks after delivery, your hormones begin to deplete. Unfortunately, so does your hair! It's falling out everywhere: it's in the brush, at the bottom of the shower, on your sweater, in the car seat, at the office.

Thankfully, your hair won't look thinner than usual. During your pregnancy, your hair was lush and growing like mad; so now, you actually have more hair to lose. To give you an idea of how much hair you'll lose, before pregnancy, you lost an average of 125 strands of hair per day. After delivery, you may lose about 500 strands of hair a day!

But relax—you're not going bald. The hair will stop falling out.

Concerns about Your Vaginal Discharge

A bloody vaginal discharge called *lochia* is a normal part of recovering from childbirth. (See page 137 for more on lochia.) "Over four to six weeks postpartum, it will become thinner and pinkish, and eventually yellowish," says maternal/child nurse and lactation consultant Beth Iovinelli. You only need to be concerned if your bleeding remains heavy or bright red. How much discharge is too much? If you are soaking a sanitary pad every hour, call your healthcare provider: that's too much blood. The best way to ease the bleeding is to rest. If you're on your feet and trying to accomplish too much, you may experience heavier bleeding. It's your body's way of telling you to slow down.

Give Your Body a Rest

To avoid infection, don't use tampons, douche, have sex, or immerse yourself in water (sitz baths are OK) for six weeks after delivery, or until your healthcare provider says it's all right.

Going to the Bathroom

If the thought of having a bowel movement seems daunting after delivery, try taking a stool softener—it will ease the pain. Your doctor or midwife can prescribe one that's appropriate.

The Postpregnancy Blues

Feeling a little blue? Blame it on the hormones! When my son was one month old, I used to get teary-eyed even at the thought of him growing up and finding another woman! He was going to leave me and get married . . . and I might not even like her!

It's OK and perfectly normal to feel weepy, slightly depressed, and overwhelmed just after giving birth. Your pregnancy hormones are still taking you for quite a ride!

In order to combat the postpregnancy blues, you need to have a plan. Here are some tips that can help.

- Take time to relax and do things for yourself. Sleep, go for a walk, go into town, or curl up with a good book.
- If you can, get help with laundry, vacuuming, food shopping, and meals.
- Now is not the time to be a perfectionist. To avoid feelings of failure, keep your lists and projects to a bare minimum.
- Don't spend too much time alone. If the weather is nice, spend time outside at a park or walking with the baby in a stroller.

- Participate in a support group for new moms. These are offered through the hospital or your pediatrician's office.
- Surround yourself with a core team of support. This team should supply you with physical help, good advice, and a non-judgmental shoulder to cry on.

If you are feeling severely anxious and depressed, *don't hesitate to call your healthcare provider*. You may be experiencing postpartum depression. Don't feel bad or stigmatized, for many women have this problem! It can be treated, and it only gets worse if left untreated.

Leaving the House with Your Baby

There is nothing more exciting than showing off your newborn baby. And if you're a working mom, it's always fun to visit your colleagues. So don't be too disappointed if your pediatrician bans such visits until your newborn is at least three months old. The amount of time that you should stay away from indoor public places may vary from one pediatrician to another. But in general, it's always best to err on the side of caution. Your newborn is more susceptible to viruses and bacteria than other people are, so of course, it's best to avoid them. Never visit with anyone who is sick or who has a cold, and do not feel uncomfortable about having everyone wash their hands before holding your baby. My son was born in August, so we spent a lot of time outside and went to restaurants that had outdoor seating. A baby who is born in the middle of flu season may be spending a little more time at home.

Flying with Your Baby

Don't plan on air travel right away, but once you have the go-ahead from your pediatrician, air travel is perfectly safe for your little one. Just be prepared for some fussing during takeoff and landing, when your baby's ears are being bothered by the change in cabin pressure. To help clear her ears, let her suck on a pacifier or a bottle, or try breastfeeding.

Taking Car Trips

Car travel can be easy with a newborn. If you're lucky, your baby will sleep for most of the trip. Just plan on frequent stops for feedings and diaper changes. I've known a few talented women who manage to breastfeed safely while riding in the backseat. Remember to keep the baby securely in his car seat and your seat belt on.

Going Back to Work

I was so distraught about going back to work and leaving my baby. The mere thought of it would bring me to tears. It really is one of the most physically unnatural things for a new mother to do. You've spent all this time nurturing and protecting your child and then, all of a sudden, you're going to leave him under the care of someone else?

Under the haze of pregnancy hormones, it's almost too much to bear at times. I was a complete wreck, even running out of a prospective day care center in tears a month after giving birth to Jimmy. I was wracked with guilt and sadness.

Fortunately, my cousin Megan talked some sense into me. She advised me to stop wasting the precious time that I *did* have with my baby worrying, and to start enjoying every day. She told me to live in the moment and enjoy each minute with my son. I did just that! I enjoyed every second with him, and when it was time to go back to work, the hormones had lifted and it wasn't nearly as bad as I'd feared.

Easing the Transition to Work

Here are a few things that will help ease the way if you're planning on going back to work.

- Before you start back, try to do a few "dress rehearsals" and establish a morning routine that you feel comfortable with.
- If you can, start your first week back on a Thursday. Having a shorter work week will help with your transition.
- Even better, see whether your employer will allow you to start back part-time for the first few weeks.
- If you are breastfeeding, talk to a lactation consultant about pumping and storing milk, starting several weeks before returning to work.

- Talk to other working mothers. They can share tips and offer support.

- To prevent spitup from running down your suit, wear your bathrobe over your work clothes until you walk out the door!

- To ease your anxiety, leave a recording of your voice with your baby's caregiver for the baby to listen to throughout the day. You can also leave a photo album with your picture in it, or a home video for your baby to watch.

Getting Back to Sex

After all the action during delivery, the episiotomy, and the residual soreness, I was hesitant even to go to the bathroom. Once I got over that, I was not looking forward to my six-week postdelivery checkup. I wanted to be left alone!

The good news for many women, whether you had a vaginal birth or a C-section, is that you must postpone sex for at least six weeks after delivery. Your uterus and cervix need time to heal, and the introduction of foreign bacteria could cause infection. Episiotomy stitches are another reason to go easy—you don't want to tear them.

When you feel ready for sex, check with your healthcare provider. He or she can give you the go-ahead.

Making Sex More Comfortable

Even after your healthcare provider has given you the green light, you may be nervous about how intercourse will feel. Some women who breastfeed experience vaginal dryness from a change in hormone levels, or maybe you had an episiotomy and you still feel occasional soreness. Try using a lubricant—it can make a big difference. There are a number of lubricating gels and liquids on the market (different from contraceptive gels!), and you can find them in your local drugstore.

Dads and Bonding

Don't be upset if your husband or partner does not establish an immediate bond with his new baby. Although he loves his new baby more than anything in this world, the care and natural instincts to handle an infant may seem foreign to him. Some fathers are great with newborns, while others do a little better with an older baby. There are ways that a dad can bond and feel involved. Letting the baby suck on his finger, keeping plenty of skin-to-skin contact, and swaying and rocking always do the trick. So do baby slings.

I'll never forget the day my husband truly bonded with our son. I had had a sleepless night and was at wit's end one morning when I realized that my husband's routine hadn't changed one bit! How could I tell? He was in our makeshift gym, on the Stairmaster, enjoying a workout! I placed our son in the infant car seat, plopped it at the bottom of the Stairmaster, and left. And I mean, *I left the house!*

My husband had no choice but to interact and cope, so . . . on went the baby sling and out the door they went, two boys going for a hike. During that hike, my husband realized that not only did he have a son, but he also had a new playmate. He fell madly in love with his new best buddy.

Being a Good Parent

"Will I be a good mom?" "Do I have what it takes to care for an infant?" It's natural to question yourself when you undertake such an immense task, but all you really need is love—and a lot of it. Keep your home safe and happy, with a stimulating environment where your baby's needs are tended to. Sing, talk, dance, read, and laugh—and have a lot of fun!

LEARNING YOUR BABY'S BODY

Caring for the Umbilical Cord

If you forget to clean the cord with alcohol, don't worry; you're not a bad mother. Clean and dry cords will fall off at about the same rate as a cord that is swabbed with alcohol. Just watch for signs of infection (redness around the umbilical cord, and any drainage). Call your healthcare provider if infection occurs.

Don't Be Scared of the Soft Spots

It's OK to gently massage the two soft spots, or *fontanelles*, while washing your baby's hair. These spots are protected under the skin by a tough, canvaslike membrane called the *dura.*

At birth, your baby's skull bones were relatively soft and connected by tissue. They're designed like this for a reason: when your baby passes through the birth canal, her head is able to mold into more of a cone shape as the bones slide over each other. Over time, the bones join together, and the two soft spots will slowly disappear. The posterior *fontanelle,* on the back of your baby's head, takes just eight to twelve weeks to close; the anterior *fontanelle,* toward the front of her head, takes eighteen months.

Caring for Delicate Infant Skin

A baby's porcelain skin is very sensitive. In the womb, it was protected by the amniotic fluid. Now that your baby is being exposed to perfumes and detergents for the first time, it's very common for rashes to occur. One of the most common rashes is called *newborn rash*: tiny white-heads, surrounded by a reddened area, that can be found anywhere on the body. The baby may also have little white dots (called *milia*) on the face and nose. Let them be, and they'll go as quickly as they came. A baby's skin heals remarkably fast.

To help protect your baby's delicate skin, Beth Iovinelli recommends using Cetaphil cleansing liquid. It's so mild, you don't have to worry about it leaving a drying, soapy residue on your baby's skin.

Tips for Cutting Nails

What could be sweeter than a newborn's delicate little fingers? You wouldn't think that their cute little nails could do so much damage. The morning of my son's christening, I was shocked to see a scratched and clawed little face peering out of his crib. He did a number on himself—perfect for all the photos we took that day!

Trimming your baby's nails can be a daunting task. It's best to wait until he is sedated with milk, or better yet, asleep. You can use a soft, baby-size emery board to file his nails; or, if you're using a baby nail clipper, hold his finger and push the nail bed away from the nail you're trimming.

How to Control Cradle Cap

I'd always heard of cradle cap, but I'd never seen it. Then, one morning, I was nursing my son and stroking his hair when I realized that his entire scalp was covered with a crusty, hardened scab of dead skin. Sound pleasant?

Thanks to Beth Iovinelli, I knew what to do. She had told me to brush the flakes away with a firm-bristled brush. So, I began brushing, and soon he looked like the Abominable Snowman in *Rudolph the Red-Nosed Reindeer*. His hair was sticking straight up, and it looked like a blizzard of snow had landed on top of his head! How was I going to get all those flakes out? I carefully washed Jimmy's hair a couple of times with Head and Shoulders dandruff shampoo, and soon it was back to normal.

"Why Is My Baby Flinching?"

After spending nine months in your womb, your baby is used to being in a very small, cramped space. That's why the swaddle or "burrito wrap" technique they teach you in the hospital is so comforting to babies. When your baby isn't wrapped, you may notice that her arms, legs, and even clenched fists spasm from time to time—almost as if she thinks she's falling. This is called the *startle reflex,* and it can also happen in response to a loud or sudden noise. This is a normal stage for an infant, and it can last a couple of weeks to a few months.

That is also why babies cry while being bathed: they miss the confinement and hate the sudden exposure. Beth Iovinelli taught me this trick: when your newborn is crying during a bath, hold his arms close to his chest. The crying will almost immediately subside.

Your Baby's Breathing

If you're not prepared for how fast an infant breathes, you may be alarmed when you watch how quickly his little chest pumps up and down when he's breathing. Not only does he take rapid breaths, but he may even appear not to be breathing for a few seconds. Don't panic! All of this irregular breathing will even out within a couple of weeks—your baby's lungs are just getting used to breathing outside of the womb.

A Lump in the Chest

Right after my son was born, I noticed he had a tiny, bony lump protruding from the center of his chest. To my relief, it was just his breastbone.

In some babies, it's noticeable; but it disappears completely within a few months.

Fluid in the Lungs!

The most terrifying moment I had with my newborn was within an hour of our homecoming. My husband was out running yet another errand, but my mother, thank God, was with me. The baby began to gag and choke for what seemed like an eternity. As I froze in absolute fear, my mother grabbed him and rested him on her knee as if she were burping him. After a few tense moments, he coughed up a liquidy mucus and was perfectly fine.

Before delivery, your baby's lungs are filled with fluid. During a vaginal delivery, most of this fluid is squeezed out of the lungs as the chest is compressed in the birth canal. Nurses may suction out some fluid during labor and delivery; any fluid that still remains is usually coughed up or absorbed within a few minutes.

The fluid should all be cleared out by the time you take your baby home from the hospital . . . but be aware that it might not be, and don't panic if he does need to cough up a little bit more. Just place him on his stomach on your lap, pat gently on his back, and everything will be all right.

Curved Baby Feet

One of the little-baby oddities that had me slightly concerned was that Jimmy's beautiful, tiny feet were curved inward. I worried—how was he ever going to walk? This, too, it turns out, is normal. It's believed to occur because of a lack of space in your uterus. You may even notice that your baby's legs are slightly bowed. Once he gets to stretch out and kick for a good couple of months, you'll see his feet and legs begin to straighten—and you'll be running after him in no time!

Why Your Baby's Joints Pop

You try to be so careful when you pick up your baby; but no matter how careful you are, from time to time you may hear pops and cracks from his tiny bones. Sounds bad, but it isn't at all. His bones and ligaments still have spaces between them. They'll stop popping after a couple of months, when the spaces fill in.

Blocked Tear Ducts

Waking up in the morning and going to get your cooing, bright-eyed baby from the crib is the most incredible feeling in the world! But one morning I went to get Jimmy from his crib, only to find both his eyes glued shut with a yellowy-greenish crust. He was crying—I hate to imagine how panicked *he* must have felt. But I tried to remain calm because in the back of my mind, I knew it was a severe case of the sandman. I soaked a cotton ball in warm water and gently massaged his eyes, dislodging the crust that had formed.

After a visit to the doctor later that day, we discovered that Jimmy had a blocked tear duct. It's common in infants, and it makes their eyes very watery and teary in appearance. This can also leave a baby prone to conjunctivitis. After a couple of days of eyedrops and massaging the tear-duct passage, his conjunctivitis cleared, and he was my bright-eyed beautiful boy once again.

Flat Heads and How to Prevent Them

The cause of sudden infant death syndrome (SIDS) remains a bit of a mystery in the medical community; but thanks to the "back-to-sleep" campaign that was launched by the American Academy of Pediatrics in 1992, there has been a large reduction in deaths in the past decade.

SIDS has, in fact, dropped by 40 percent since the campaign launched. (For more on SIDS, see page 100.)

The back-to-sleep campaign stressed the importance of having babies sleep on their backs. One minor consequence of this is that they have a tendency to develop a flat head from sleeping in this position. Don't panic; it's not permanent! To avoid a flat head, alternate the direction of your baby's head when you put him to sleep or while he's in the car seat.

On the flip side, tummy time is in! During waking hours, a fun exercise for your baby is to lay her on her stomach and have her work on her chest, upper back, and neck muscles. By trying to lift her body and neck off the floor, she's getting a tremendous workout! For an added benefit, place her on your husband's or partner's chest and let her go to work. It's a great bonding experience for both of them.

Suddenly Appearing Birthmarks

Don't be alarmed if, one day, you discover a red, raised mark on your baby. Just ask your pediatrician—it's most likely a birthmark. Many babies are not born with birthmarks, but birthmarks can appear a week or two after birth. It's the last thing you're expecting to see, so it can be very shocking. My friend Isabelle went to change her son one day and found a red mark on his shoulder. Convinced it was a blood clot, she rushed him to the hospital only to find it was a common birthmark.

Although they are common, the exact cause of birthmarks is not known. They most likely result from the abnormal development of blood vessels. Some marks are with you for life, while others fade away over time.

SANE MOMMY PHILOSOPHY

Why Babies Cry

"The baby didn't cry like this in the hospital! What's wrong?" Probably nothing at all. Crying is your baby's only method of communicating with you. She discovers that when she cries, you come and take care of whatever it is she needs.

Around twelve weeks of age, things will begin to quiet down a bit as your brilliant baby learns more pleasant ways of communicating, such as cooing and smiling. These new techniques will take care of certain needs, and she'll save the cries for the big stuff . . . like being fed!

Some babies will cry for no reason at all in the late afternoon and early evening—precisely the time when you're the most tired and trying to get dinner ready. Some say it's an infant's way of winding down and getting ready for sleep. If you can, don't fight it and get frustrated. Instead, spend that time with your baby outside in a stroller or at a park. The fresh air will help you both unwind.

"Which Cry Is This?"

A lot of baby books talk about the necessity of interpreting your infant's cries. I have to admit, I found it slightly frustrating. I had no idea what each different cry meant. They all sounded the same to me! And each sweet little cry caused a shooting jolt of anxiety . . . "What could he want this time? Is this one a hungry cry, which is different from a tired cry, which is different from a boredom cry, which is different from an

I-need-my-diaper-changed cry? And what about the I'm-in-discomfort cry?"

After a short while, you do become able to distinguish the more serious cries from those that are less so, and you quickly learn to comfort your baby in either case.

Positions to Soothe a Newborn

If you have a fussy, cranky newborn, try putting her on her side or even her stomach. That is always a more soothing position than placing her on her back, where she feels open, exposed, and perhaps even like she's falling. Remember, this is just a temporary way to soothe a baby; when she's ready for a nap, put her on her back to prevent sudden infant death syndrome (SIDS). If she's wrapped snugly, she'll feel safe and secure.

The Myth of the Quiet Nursery

Don't spend needless time trying to keep everyone quiet while your newborn is sleeping. Your baby has been able to hear the barking dog, the vacuum cleaner, and other household noises since twenty-four weeks. And your womb itself was a very noisy place—the swooshing of blood, the gurgling of your stomach, and the constant motion while you walked were all very comforting to your baby. So, go ahead and rock, bounce, jostle, and swoosh your newborn to sleep. You'll find it works much better than a quiet, still crib.

Don't Rush a Routine

Don't be too concerned about your baby's napping and eating routine: it will emerge when he's ready. Other mothers would confidently talk about their infants' routines, and I couldn't possibly make sense of my son's twenty-four-hour sleeping and eating extravaganza! What were they talking about? We didn't have anything that resembled a routine. I let it go, and one day, out of the blue, I realized something that resembled a routine was beginning to emerge. All the chaos does fall into place eventually. To start easing your baby toward a routine, give him a bath every night at the same time, or take him on a daily morning walk in the stroller. You'll begin to see the naps and feeding schedules fall into place.

Take Your Baby Outdoors

A little bit of sunshine can do wonders for your baby's disposition. It's a natural high that stimulates serotonin, dopamine, and beta-endorphins—all naturally occurring chemicals that make you happy. The sun is also nature's best source of vitamin D: the skin absorbs the ultraviolet rays and converts them to a healthy dose of vitamin D. And it can even help decrease jaundice.

Of course, you should expose your baby to direct sunlight for only very short periods of time in the early morning or late afternoon, when the sun is not too strong. Although sunscreen is essential when out in the sun, avoid using it on your baby's delicate skin until she's six months old. Don't forget a hat!

Avoid Midnight Diaper Changes

My friend Ronit shared this piece of advice with me: don't feel that you always have to change wet diapers in the middle of the night. When your baby finally starts to sleep through the night, are you going to wake him to change a diaper? Of course not!

Don't Compare Babies

It's nice to chat with other mothers; they're a great resource. But be careful when comparing your baby's development with theirs—it can stress you out unnecessarily. All babies develop at their own pace, and a lot of the early differences will even out over time.

Different Stages

Always remember, a stage is just a stage. While it may be difficult, it will pass in a few short weeks! For my husband and me, the umbilical cord care added extra stress during diaper changes for those first ten days after we brought our son home from the hospital. (When you're operating on limited sleep, your tolerance for stress is very low . . . at least mine was!) It seemed like forever waiting for the little, black, shriveled stump to fall off! Finally, exactly ten days later, it fell off. But to my surprise, I couldn't find it anywhere. I was looking all over the changing table. Finally, when I walked in and told my husband that the umbilical cord had fallen off but I couldn't find it, guess what he said? "It's right there, stuck to your nightgown!"

You Can't Spoil an Infant

How many times have you debated this question with a family member? I know I did. But the bottom line is, you can't spoil an infant.

For the first six months of your baby's life, the word *spoil* does not exist! If you respond quickly to your baby's needs, twenty-four hours a day, he will develop trust and grow up to be a secure child, knowing that his parents will always be there for him. However, don't worry if your child is crying and you can't respond right away. It's OK to leave him in a safe place while you change a load of laundry or answer the phone.

And if your baby has been fussy all day, don't worry about taking a five-minute timeout for yourself. You're going to be a better and more patient mom after you've been recharged!

Don't Feel Bad When You're Busy

It's impossible to entertain an infant twenty-four hours a day. Human touch and interaction are critical to your baby's development, but it's just as important to teach your infant how to entertain himself. So, don't feel guilty letting him sit by himself watching a mobile, listening to music, or just looking out a window. He's being amused, and you get to take a break.

The Benefits of Babysitting

You need time to yourself to rejuvenate, recharge, and *not* be on call. It's probably one of the most difficult things for a new mother to do—to leave your precious newborn in the care of someone else. But you *must* try it, and you *must* do it early on, to get over your fears. I'm not talking about dinner and a movie within the first two weeks, although some women do feel comfortable with that. I mean having a family member or close friend watch the baby for an hour in between feedings while you integrate yourself into society again. Go for a cup of coffee, or buy yourself a treat . . . you deserve it! It may feel a little weird at first to see that life still goes on outside the four walls of your home. But it's important for your own psychological health—and that affects your baby directly.

Be sure to reassure your sitter, whether it's your mother-in-law or best friend, that you fully trust her and you know she's competent. It will make you both feel better!

BREASTFEEDING 101

Gearing Up for Breastfeeding

Breastfeeding is great for your baby, and it's good for you, too. Breast milk jump-starts your baby's immune system and provides protection against ear infections, diarrhea, allergies, asthma, and childhood obesity. Breastfeeding also decreases your risk of developing breast and ovarian cancer and, possibly, osteoporosis. It reduces your risk of postpartum depression and even helps you lose your baby weight sooner. It's amazing how long the benefits last!

It may take a few weeks before you remember all these benefits, though. The first few days of breastfeeding can be especially tough. I wasn't expecting it to be so hard and mentally draining. The good news is, *you can do it*—and it's the most rewarding job you'll ever have! As with the rest of childbearing, it goes much better if you have information, support, and an open outlook.

You Need a Support Network!

If there's one thing I want you to take from this breastfeeding chapter, it's this: *Get yourself a support network!* The more support you have from others, the longer you're likely to breastfeed, and the easier your transition into motherhood will be.

Support from Other Moms

Attend a breastfeeding support group or new mothers' group; many hospitals and some community centers offer them. Or you can contact

La Leche League, which runs support groups worldwide and even online (go to www.lalecheleague.org or call 1-800-LALECHE).

There are so many benefits to joining a group. Many hospital-based groups are run by lactation consultants who can troubleshoot and coach you when the going gets rough. La Leche League also trains its leaders in breastfeeding education. Just as important as the experts are the other moms: you'll pick up lots of tips and ideas to use at home, and you may even make some friends for life. This is a great way to develop a peer group, especially if you're new to the area or staying home from work for the first time.

Support at Home

Support on the home front is another key to successful breastfeeding. Perhaps the biggest role your husband or partner can play is paying close attention to the advice from your nurse or lactation consultant immediately after you give birth. It's very hard for a sleep-deprived new mom to retain all the information that she is being inundated with, and it will help him feel more involved if he can act as your "consultant" when you return home.

You'll also need his support during those sleepless, hormone-laden days immediately after birth. I didn't realize it at the time, but my husband really paid attention to every word of Beth Iovinelli's advice. When we got home, he stepped up to the plate and took an active role in Jimmy's feeding. He helped keep track of the breastfeeding journal (see page 196) for those first two weeks by writing in when, how long, and which breast for each feeding. Having that kind of support made my job a whole lot easier.

Keeping an Open Outlook

Successful breastfeeding requires a change in your perspective. Your baby's body will tell her what she needs, and your job right now is to respond. "Once you come to terms with the fact that you are open for business twenty-four hours and there is no putting the baby 'to bed,' you are ahead of the game," explains Beth Iovinelli. You may feel overwhelmed at first, but don't panic! In difficult moments, call on your support network. You are not alone! And rest assured, breastfeeding does get easier: generally, after about six weeks, most women start to feel much more confident with breastfeeding.

"How Can My Body Possibly Produce Enough Milk?"

I had moments when I was in complete awe that my body had actually produced another human being! And I was equally amazed that my small breasts could actually *feed* this child. He would live, and thrive, on my breast milk! But could my body really do it? Yes. Here's how the amazing process works.

After delivery, the placenta detaches from the uterine wall, signaling your body to start producing milk. It will take a couple of days for your milk to come in, but don't panic—your baby will not go hungry. Beth Iovinelli reassured me of this when I was in the hospital. Here's what she says:

> While you're waiting for your milk to come in, your baby will be satisfied with your colostrum. At each feeding, your baby will get about one to two tablespoons of this high-protein pre-milk. This is plenty for your newborn's small stomach capacity! These small feedings also give your baby a chance to negotiate latching, sucking, and swallowing. By the time your milk comes in, your baby will be more alert, with a bigger appetite, and ready for a bountiful milk supply. Also, your baby is born well-hydrated (just look at those puffy eyes!). This can compensate for the smaller amounts of fluid (colostrum) in your breasts for those first few days.

It's a wonderful comfort when you actually see your body producing milk. Beth came to check on us in our hospital room and asked if Jimmy and I were ready for our first feeding. She took hold of my breast and began to gently express the creamy yellow drops of colostrum, right before my eyes. I was thrilled, amazed, and, of course, relieved. Seeing *is* believing!

Feed on One Breast Thoroughly

When you first begin to breastfeed, don't be concerned about switching your baby from breast to breast during a feeding. Keep it simple, and let the baby feed on one breast from start to finish.

Beth Iovinelli suggests, "After the baby comes off the first breast after a period of active eating, burp her, and then offer the second breast. It's OK if she doesn't want it at this point."

By keeping your baby on one breast longer (rather than feeling compelled to go for both breasts), you can ensure that she gets all the right "components" of milk. First, she gets the *foremilk,* which is like skim milk—it's watery and is designed to quench your baby's thirst. Then, a richer, fattier milk called *hindmilk* follows the foremilk. It has the consistency of cream. The hindmilk satisfies your baby's hunger and is high in calories, which helps your baby put on weight. Think of it as your baby's dessert.

Cramps during Feedings

After your baby is delivered, you're left with a rather large uterus. Your uterus, which weighed roughly two ounces before you became pregnant, now weighs close to a pound! How does it shrink back to its regular size? As soon as your baby latches on to your breast and begins to feed, your body releases oxytocin, which causes your uterus to shrink back to its normal size. This process can give you mild, menstrual-type cramps.

What to Do When Your Milk Comes In

You may be home from the hospital by the time your milk comes in, but believe me, you'll know when it does! Some women experience mild engorgement, while others get very full. In addition to your milk, there is extra blood flow and fluid in your breast tissue.

Some women's breasts become so engorged with milk that they look and feel like melons. Imagine your infant trying to latch on to a rock-hard melon! Of course, a softer, more giving breast and nipple will make it much easier for your baby to latch on.

Easing Breast Engorgement

- Before feeding, place warm compresses directly on your breasts or take a warm shower. The warmth increases circulation and helps the milk to flow. Now you can hand-express some milk, which softens your breasts and makes it easier for your baby to latch on.

- After feeding, Beth Iovinelli recommends using cold compresses. They slow down your milk flow and help keep your breasts from becoming engorged. Here's a trick that worked for me: keep a head of cabbage in your refrigerator. After breastfeeding, peel off a leaf, wash it, and then place it inside your bra. Not only is it cool and soothing, but it actually contains a chemical that helps with fluid reabsorption! And it soothes sore nipples, too. *Note:* Stay away from the cabbage if you're allergic to sulfa, and don't try this if your nipples are cracked or bleeding.

What You Can Do about Sore Nipples

Even with a "textbook" latch, breastfeeding moms may experience some nipple tenderness. How much tenderness you experience depends on how well you get the baby latched on. Don't panic: some soreness is normal, and it will pass as your nipples get used to your new little vacuum cleaner! In the meantime, it may help to apply a pure lanolin breast cream such as Lansinoh or PureLan 100.

If your nipples remain sore for an extended period and your baby seems very cranky, you may have a poor latch. To avoid a poor latch, which can cause severe tenderness, make sure that the baby is approaching the breast with an open mouth and that he has his mouth around a large portion of the areola (the dark area around the nipple). Beth Iovinelli explains it like this: "Think of a tube of toothpaste. You get more from squeezing the tube [the areola] than you would from squeezing the tip of the toothpaste tube [the nipple alone]." If you try this tip and you're still having trouble, see a lactation consultant: she can help you get things back on track.

"Is This Kid Eating or Playing?"

Some babies like to play around at the breast. Suckling is really soothing to a baby, even if there's no milk involved. To figure out whether your baby is eating or playing, listen for swallowing and watch how deeply his jaw is moving. Most babies will suck differently when they're sucking for comfort.

Too Many Bowel Movements?

Don't panic if your baby seems to poop a lot. A baby on formula poops three or four times a day.

There is a natural laxative in breast milk, so a breastfed baby will poop more often—on average, two to five times a day.

Write Down Feedings and Diaper Changes

Breastfeeding your baby can be stressful at first. There's the issue of whether she'll latch on or not; and then, if she does, it's hard to tell whether she's getting enough milk. One way to help ease your mind is to keep a breastfeeding journal for the first two weeks. Write down when your baby ate, for how long, and on which breast.

Keep a diaper journal, too—a record of the daily number of wet and soiled diapers. Look for six to eight wet diapers and two to five bowel movements daily, beginning the third day after birth. Be sure to note the color of the bowel movements: They'll start out black; then by the second day, they'll go to brown; by the third day, to green; and finally, depending on whether you're formula feeding or breastfeeding, they'll become either yellow and mushy (if breastfed) or anywhere from pale yellow to light brown with a slightly harder consistency (if formula-fed). They will remain that color until you start your baby on solid food at four to five months of age.

Your diaper journal can be an invaluable tool when you're talking to your pediatrician or lactation consultant. If there are any questions or concerns about your baby's weight gain, hydration, or digestion, the journal can help them evaluate what is going on.

Once you feel comfortable with your baby's routine, you can throw out the journal and relax!

Breastfeeding Soothes Baby's First Shot

Yet another reason why breastfeeding is great: it can help to reduce the stinging pain from those horrible vaccinations! The combination of your touch, skin, and smell, and the taste of your milk, helps to comfort your baby. You can try feeding her during the shots or immediately afterward. It may help you feel better, too.

"My Baby Eats All the Time. Is This a Bad Habit?"

There are no rules or manuals for your baby! Let your baby guide you. As long as you are listening and responding to his needs, you're not doing anything wrong. If he ate an hour ago and wants to eat again, go for it! Although this constant eating may wear you down a bit, it does give comfort and helps establish a good milk supply.

There's another reason for all this eating: very young babies have small stomachs that can't hold much food at a time. Newborns may nurse every two hours, and that's counting from the beginning of one feeding to the beginning of the next. Slightly older babies will eat every two to three hours. Beth Iovinelli says to wake your baby for a feeding at the three-hour mark if he's still asleep.

Do Your Thank-You Notes While Feeding

If your baby is a constant eater, there are ways to make the best of it. One is to write your thank-you notes during feedings. When you're ready to feed on your "non-writing" side, settle yourself in an armchair at the kitchen table with a pillow under that arm, and use your good hand to write.

"My Milk Is Drying Up!"

If you feel that your milk supply is running low, don't panic, but do call a lactation consultant right away. She can help you determine what is happening and arm you with a plan to pick your milk supply back up. To find a lactation consultant, call your hospital, OB/GYN, pediatrician, or the La Leche League.

Things that may help rejuvenate your milk supply include lots of fluids, nutritious foods, adequate rest, and skin-to-skin contact with your baby.

Dealing with a Slow Eater

Some babies like to eat fast, and others like to take their time. I remember sitting on the couch and watching an entire Oprah show on television while my baby breastfed . . . and that was just one side! Is this normal? Yes, it is. You just have a slow eater.

It's perfectly normal for a baby to take as little as five minutes or as much as an hour to complete eating. When you allow your baby to set the pace, he develops an internal appetite control that tells him when he's full. Don't worry; your baby will also become a more efficient eater after a few weeks.

Constant Feeding and Growth Spurts

When your baby is about three weeks old, you can expect his first growth spurt. He may be a fixture at your breast for at least two days. If you give him full rein and unlimited access to your breast, he'll be able to increase your milk supply to meet his demand for extra calories. After the growth spurt passes, he'll settle back into a more predictable feeding pattern.

Rather than fight it, spend these long feeds enjoying your baby, and let the dirty dishes and the laundry wait. Or pick up a good book or magazine to read while breastfeeding. If he's tucked into bed beside you, you may find yourself dozing off and getting some much-needed rest.

In a month or so, you'll find that he's easily distracted, and you'll wonder whether he's getting enough to eat after just five minutes at the breast! *Don't panic*—he's become such an efficient eater that it takes him less time to fill up now.

Expect more growth spurts around the sixth and twelfth weeks. He may be fussy until your milk supply catches up with his ravenous appetite.

"I'm So Thirsty!"

Listen to your body. It knows exactly what it's doing—even though you may not! The second your baby latches on and takes one good swallow of milk, your mouth turns to cotton balls. Why? Your body is reminding you that it needs water to produce milk. When you're breastfeeding, you should be drinking at least eight to twelve eight-ounce glasses of water a day! To help remind me to drink water, I placed bottles of water at all my breastfeeding stations throughout the house; by my bed, next to the couch, in our living room, and in the baby's nursery next to the rocking chair. Also keep a bowl of fruit, tissues, and some reading material on hand for those marathon feedings.

Producing Too Much Milk

Too much milk may not always be a good thing! It can cause problems in a couple of ways.

If you have a large milk supply, your baby may be getting too much of the watery foremilk and not enough of the fatty hindmilk. Too much foremilk can cause gas, leaving your baby with an upset stomach or even diarrhea. (You can actually see a difference between foremilk and hindmilk: Foremilk is more watery than hindmilk and a little bluish in color; hindmilk looks more like cream.)

Beth Iovinelli explains another issue with too much milk: "Babies may pull away and cry soon after starting to breastfeed. The letdown, or release, of milk can be too strong and fast, causing a sudden 'gush.'"

If your baby seems overly fussy, Beth suggests working with a lactation consultant, because "this can be a multifaceted issue. Also, feed from only one breast. If the baby is ready to feed again before three to four hours, put her back on the same breast. This repeat feeding allows her to get to the hindmilk. You may have to express some milk from the other breast to prevent engorgement while you're feeding twice or even three times in a row on the same breast."

A Blister on Baby's Lip

Don't be alarmed if you notice a tiny blister or a patch of dry skin develop on your baby's upper lip. These are called sucking blisters; they get their name from your baby's ability to suck like a little vacuum! They're not painful to your baby, so just let them be and they'll disappear on their own, which could take up to a year.

Spitup

Breast milk was like liquid gold. I hated to see a drop of it wasted! I was always a little discouraged when, after a great feeding session, Jimmy's burp would leave milk on my shoulder and running down my back. I also wondered: Did that mean I had to feed him again? How could I, when he had just drained both breasts? The truth is, spitup looks like a lot more volume than it is. On average, it's only a teaspoonful.

Why does spitup happen? Your ravenous little eater spits up formula or breast milk because while he's sucking, he's also taking in air, which forms little air pockets in and around the milk. When that air comes up in the form of a burp, so does a little milk. Around six months of age, the spitting-up phase is finally behind you.

Avoiding Spitup Sessions

Give these techniques a try:

- Burp your baby and burp him again . . . especially during those late-night feedings, no matter how tired you are. A rough gauge is to burp every three ounces for a bottle-fed baby, and between breasts for a breastfed baby.

- Make sure the nipple is the right one for the age of your baby. If the hole is too big, your baby will take in too much air with his milk.

- The less activity after eating, the better. Also, both before and directly after feeding, keep gravity on your side by placing your baby in an up-right postion.

If Your Baby Has Reflux

Reflux can keep your baby from getting a good night's sleep. My friend Suzy shared this tip: "My son had reflux from very early on. We had him sleep upright in his car seat until he was almost six months old. He slept through the night, and so did we."

Alcohol and Breastfeeding

When you drink alcohol, some of it passes into your breast milk. How quickly it metabolizes out of your body (and your milk) and how it will affect your baby depends on a lot of individual factors. While nobody recommends drinking regularly when you're breastfeeding, the occasional, single drink does not appear to harm a breastfed baby or a mother's milk supply.

If you choose to indulge in the occasional single drink, make sure you know how to measure it. One drink equals a 5-ounce glass of wine, a 12-ounce beer, or 1½ ounces of hard (80-proof) liquor, total—whether in a cocktail or by itself. To minimize the impact on your child, Beth Iovinelli offers this simple rule of thumb: "Feed the baby, have your one drink with dinner, and by the time the baby is ready to nurse again (at least two hours later), the alcohol will likely have metabolized its way out of your system."

Don't Drink and Co-Sleep

If you or your partner have had even one alcoholic drink, or if either of you is taking any medication that leads to sleepiness, *do not put your baby in bed with you.* In your heavy sleep, you could accidentally roll over and hurt your precious little one.

Medications and Breastfeeding

Many medications are actually safe to take while breastfeeding. Some medications metabolize out of your breast milk within a few hours; others do not. Check with your healthcare provider, certified lactation consultant, or pediatrician for the latest advice on specific medications and when to take them. *Medications and Mother's Milk*, by Thomas Hale, PhD (Pharmasoft Medical Publishing, 2004), is a great reference work on this subject.

Herbs and Breastfeeding

The Nursing Mother's Herbal, by registered nurse and lactation consultant Sheila Humphrey (Fairview Press, 2004), is a great reference on breastfeeding and the use of herbs.

Choosing and Using a Breast Pump

If you plan to return to work and you want to continue breastfeeding for an extended period of time (the World Health Organization recommends breastfeeding for at least a year), you should invest in a good electric breast pump. Medela is one reputable brand. Choose a model with a double pump, so you can pump both breasts at the same time. An efficient pump will make your life a whole lot easier: you can finish pumping in as little as fifteen minutes! A good-quality pump will also come with usage and milk storage instructions, or you can ask a lactation consultant for help.

If you plan to return to work, start using the pump beforehand, to ease the transition. Wait until you've been breastfeeding for at least a month. "You want to first establish your milk supply and get good at breastfeeding," says Beth Iovinelli. Once you've gone back to work, to help maintain your milk supply, breastfeed the baby whenever you are home: before leaving for work, when you return home, and during the middle of the night.

Be Patient about Pumping

Don't panic about learning to use a breast pump—it's not as hard as it looks! I planned to go back to work after four months, and I was so anxious to figure out my breast pump that I brought it with me to the hospital at delivery time, hoping for a lesson. No such luck! Beth Iovinelli told me to put it away for at least a month, until my milk supply and my baby's latch-on technique were well established.

Once my milk supply was established and Jimmy and I had become pros at breastfeeding, I made my first pumping attempt. It was pathetic. I pumped for ten minutes on each breast, and all I got was a couple of ounces. I wondered, "How am I going to continue to feed my son breast milk when it's time to go back to work?" Beth told me to be patient and keep trying; pumping can be an adjustment for some women. And sure enough, with time, I was pumping plenty of milk!

Tips for Pumping at Work

Pumping milk at work has become commonplace. There's no need to feel uncomfortable about it!

- Some electric pumps come in discreet shoulder bags that blend right in with your purse, computer bag, or briefcase.
- Look for a quiet, private place where you can sit for fifteen to twenty minutes; some companies have "quiet rooms" or lounges specifically for this purpose.

- Take along a photo of your baby. Some women find this helps them let down milk more easily.
- Keep your breast milk in the refrigerator at work, and buy a small, insulated cooler to keep it cold on the ride between work and home.

Introducing a Bottle

One key to successful breastfeeding is to wait at least four to six weeks before you introduce a bottle. Introducing one too soon can interfere with your milk supply and cause "nipple confusion" in your baby—for he may prefer a rubber nipple to yours.

When it's time to introduce the bottle, give your baby the first one, then have a husband, partner, or caregiver do it, so he gets used to taking a bottle from someone other than you.

BOTTLE FEEDING BASICS

Bonding While Bottle Feeding

Breastfeeding can create a beautiful bond between you and your baby. But if you are unable to breastfeed, you can still enjoy a strong bond with your baby. When you're bottle feeding, hold your baby snug to your chest; maximize skin-to-skin contact; and coo, caress, and look deep into your baby's eyes.

Sterilizing Bottles Is Easier than You Think

Our mothers and grandmothers may not have been so lucky, but with today's modern equipment it's easy to sterilize baby bottles and pacifiers. Make sure to separate the ring, nipple, and bottle, so that each piece gets thoroughly sanitized. Then just toss them into the dishwasher. Make sure that your dishwasher reaches a temperature of at least 180°F. You may want to sterilize six to eight bottles at a time, so you'll always have some on hand.

How to Choose a Nipple

A mother's nipple can come in many shapes and sizes. When shopping for bottle nipples, you'll notice that manufactured ones do, too. All of them are trying to achieve the design of Mother

Nature. So, how do you choose the best one for your baby? Leave it up to her. Buy a selection and see which type of nipple your baby prefers.

These three types of nipples all share similarities to a human nipple:

The expandable nipple, which looks short and stubby, has a flat top. As the baby sucks, this nipple will expand to the back of the throat just as a human nipple would.

An orthopedic nipple has an interesting shape, curved with a flat, bulb-like top. It's designed to reach deep into the back of the mouth, again similar to what the human nipple would do.

The bulb nipple is the most common type. It has an extra-wide base, like that of the areola of a human nipple. This is designed to make the baby open her mouth wide, which forms tight suction around her mouth, just as if she were breastfeeding.

The Size of the Nipple Hole

Nipples also come with different-size holes depending on your baby's age. Look for smaller holes for newborns and bigger holes for older babies. The package will indicate the size, and sometimes it even suggests an age range.

"When Should I Replace the Nipples?"

Replace nipples when they rip or become tacky to the touch. Be sure to check them every time you use them. It's good to keep a supply on hand in case you need to throw one out.

Choosing a Formula

With all the different formulas on the market, choosing the right one may seem overwhelming. There are different cagetories of formula: cow's-milk-based, soy-based, and hypoallergenic.

Some formulas are iron-fortified and others are not; and some formulas contain essential fatty acids, while others don't. *Don't panic*: your pediatrician can help you figure out which formula is best for your child.

Formulas for Traveling

Formulas come in powder form, in a liquid concentrate form that needs to be mixed with water, and as a "ready-to-feed" liquid. Powder is the least expensive, but it does take a little more preparation. The two liquid types are great to use when you're traveling or out and about.

How to Store Formula

- Prepared powders and concentrated mixes should be used within twenty-four hours of preparing the bottle. Keep all bottles in the refrigerator until you're ready to use them.

- Ready-to-feed formulas should be used within forty-eight hours of opening the can, and they should also be stored in the refrigerator.
- Once the bottle has touched your baby's lips, bacteria begins to grow. After two hours, the formula should be thrown out. Never reuse formula.

How to Warm Up a Bottle

Never warm a bottle in a microwave oven, as it can become dangerously hot or heat unevenly. You can heat bottles up the old-fashioned way (on the stove, in a pot of boiling water) or you can buy a bottle warmer at any baby store. What's great about a bottle warmer is that it automatically shuts off before becoming scalding hot.

I have to admit, on the occasions when I fed Jimmy with formula, I would mix it with room-temperature bottled water, and *I never heated it up!* When Jimmy's grandmothers would babysit, they'd let me know how sorry they felt for the "poor, deprived little boy." Actually, he was perfectly happy: he didn't even notice the difference!

ENVOI: TRUST YOURSELF!

My son has now graduated to thriving, happy, wild toddlerhood. It's true—the sleepless nights and constant worry of infancy are becoming a foggy memory, and it will happen for you, too!

But before I go, I want to share with you the most important piece of advice I know. *Have confidence in yourself as a parent*. You know exactly how to care for your baby: he is your child, and you, his mother, are the *only* person who knows *instinctually* how to take care of him. Trust yourself and your instincts—a mother's instincts are always one hundred percent right!

Motherhood is an incredibly hard, demanding job. Don't feel guilty or ashamed if you're not enjoying every second of it, as some people will tell you to do. It's just not realistic. Who can possibly enjoy every moment of a job that goes on twenty-four hours a day, seven days a week?

The great news is that each and every day, as your child grows, your knowledge, your skill, and your rewards grow, too. The love and the bond between mother and child are almost unexplainable in their magnitude. The day my son was born wasn't the best day of my life. It was exhausting, painful, and grueling—but I can't remember *ever* feeling so proud!

Capture Those Precious Moments!

You don't need all the latest, greatest technical equipment to commemorate your beautiful baby. A regular camera is all you need. Make sure your camera has the feature that automatically prints out the date on your pictures. Buy film and photo albums in bulk: you'll use them. Keep your photo albums out where they're handy, and when you get the pictures back from being developed, put them right into the albums.

Take rolls and rolls of pictures. Remember each stage and every roll of that luscious baby fat in pictures! I can't believe I'm going to say this, because I was so tired of hearing it, but *it does go by so fast!* I have six large photo albums in a wicker basket by the couch in our living room, and my husband and I love flipping through them and reminiscing. Our albums keep the past year's details just as vivid as ever— both the good and the bad!

ABOUT THE AUTHOR

Judy Morris is a freelance writer and a three-time Emmy Award–winning television producer for *Martha Stewart Living Television,* where she worked for the past ten years. Judy graduated from Lynchburg College with a major in English Literature and a minor in Writing. She lives in Weston, Connecticut, with her husband, Jim, and her two-year-old son, James Reid. As of this writing, she is in her ninth month of pregnancy with her second child.

James Reid has appeared on *Martha Stewart Living Television,* enjoying homemade baby food prepared by Martha and his mom, Judy. Judy was also on the show eight months pregnant, where she packed the essentials for her maternity bag and outfitted a changing table.

ABOUT THE CONTRIBUTORS

Beth Iovinelli, RN, BSN, IBCLC, graduated with honors in 1995 from New Mexico State University with a Bachelor of Science degree in Nursing. She is a member of Sigma Theta Tau, the nursing honor society, and she has been an International Board Certified Lactation Consultant (IBCLC) since 2001. She is a maternal/child health educator, teaching pre- and postnatal classes and working as a lactation consultant. She has been a labor and delivery nurse and a postpartum nurse at Norwalk Hospital in Connecticut since 1994.

Beth lives in Connecticut with her husband and her children, Connor, 10, and Erin, 8. She is passionate about helping women feel empowered to make wise healthcare decisions and to be proactive about their health.

Jay Ugol, MD, a board-certified obstetrician/gynecologist and a Fellow of the American College of Obstetricians and Gynecologists, received his undergraduate degree from the University of Rochester in New York in 1978 and his MD from Georgetown University School of Medicine in 1982. He completed his OB/GYN residency at the University of Colorado Health Sciences Center and Affiliated Hospitals in 1986 and has since been a board-certified practicing OB/GYN in the Norwalk (Connecticut) Hospital Community. Dr. Ugol is a member of Physicians for Women's Health, affiliated with Women's Health Connecticut, based in Avon, Connecticut, the nation's largest physician management partnership dedicated to women's health.

INDEX

A

acne, 56–58
albacore, 14
alcohol, 4, 207–8
alpha hydroxy, 59
amniotic fluid,
    123–25, 126
anxiety, 74–75
artificial sweeteners,
    25–26
aspartame, 25
aspirin, 4, 31

B

babies
    appearance of,
        135–37
    caring for, 162–73,
        181–82
babysitting, 182–83
bathing, 54–55, 166–67
beta-carotene, 23–24
birth control pills, 31–32
birthing plans, 121
birthmarks, 173
bladder control, 89
bleeding gums, 92–93
blood clots, 138–39
bottle feeding, 213–20
bowel movements,
    121–22, 150
Braxton-Hicks
    contractions, 96
breast feeding, 192–94

breast pumps, 210–13
breast surgery, 69–70
breastbones, 167–68
breastfeeding, 139–40,
　　184–85, 190–91
　alcohol and, 207–8
　breast pumps,
　　210–13
　cramps, 191
　growth spurts, 201–2
　issues, 194–201,
　　203–5
　medications and, 209
　milk production,
　　188–90
　positive outlook,
　　187–88
　spitup, 205–7
　support systems,
　　185–87
breasts, 66–71
breathing, 167

C
C-sections, 118–19
caffeine, 4, 8–9
cameras, 222–23
car seats, 98–99, 131
cheese, 16–18
chicken pox, 35–36
childbirth classes,
　　116–17
cleaning products,
　　41–42
coffee, 8–9
cold remedies, 31
conception, 4–6
confidence, 221
conjunctivitis,
　　170–71
constipation, 86, 87
CPR, 132
cradle cap, 165–66
cribs, 104
crying, 174–76

D

DEET, 43–44
deli meats, 17–18
developmental stages,
180–81
digestion, 84–87
discharge, 63, 137–39,
149–50

E

eggs, 4–6
embryo, 4–6
Equal, 25
exercise, 122–23
exhaustion, 71–74

F

fallopian tubes, 6
fatherhood, 159–60
fatigue, 71–74
fear, 119–20
feet, 169

fetal injuries, 78–79
fetal movements,
79–81
fingernails, 164–65
fish, 10–16
flu shots, 34
folic acid, 23
fontanelles, 162–63
food preparation,
11–12, 16
formula, 217–19

G

gas, 86–87
gift registries, 108–10
ginger, 21

H

hair loss, 147–49
hair treatments, 60–61
HCG hormone, 18–19
head shape, 171–72

healthcare, 27–29

heartburn, 84–85

hemorrhoids, 85–86

herbs, 10, 209

hormones, 150–52

hospital

arrival, 133–35

preparation for,
127–32

stays, 141–42

hot tubs, 55–56

I

illness, 34–36

immunizations, 35–36

indigestion, 31, 84

insect spray, 43–44

instincts, 221

intercourse, 64–65,
157–59

inverted nipples, 68

iron, 21–22

J

joints, 170

K

Kegel exercises, 65

king mackerel, 13

L

La Leche League,
68, 186

labor, 134–39

lawn chemicals, 47–48

leg cramps, 95

ligament pain, 95

linea nigra, 88

listeria, 16–17

litter boxes, 49–50

lochia, 137–39, 149

lumps, 167–68

lungs, 168–69

Lyme Disease,
45–46

M

medications, 30–32, 209
mercury, 12
morning sickness, 18–21
motherhood, 222
mouse droppings, 42–43
music, 48

N

nausea, 18–21
nipples, 68, 70, 194–95
nosebleeds, 92
nurseries, 112–15
Nutrasweet, 25

O

office equipment, 38–39
ovulation, 5

P

pain, 119–20
painting, 39–41

panic attacks, 74–75
parenting, 161
PCBs, 15–16
pets, 49–53
photographs, 222–23
polychlorinated biphenyls, 15–16
postpartum depression, 150–52
preparations
  for hospital, 127–32
  mental, 116–22
  physical, 122–27

R

resting, 150
Retin-A, 57–58
retinal esters, 24
routines, 177–79

S

saccharin, 25–26

salmon, 15–16

sanitary napkins, 125

saunas, 55–56

seafood, 10–16

seat belts, 79

self-tanning creams, 58

shark, 13

shellfish, 10–16

shortness of breath,
     93–94

SIDS, 100–101,
     171–72

skin care, 163–64

sleeping, 81–82, 99,
     101–3, 177

spitup, 205–7

Splenda, 25

spotting, 62–63

startle reflex,
     166–67

stress, 37–38

stretch marks, 88

Sudden Infant
     Death Syndrome,
     100–101,
     171–72

supplies, 97–99,
     104–11

support systems,
     143–44, 185–87

swelling, 90–91

swordfish, 13

T

tea, 10

tear ducts, 170–71

teeth whitening, 61

thank-you notes,
     146, 199

tilefish, 13

time management,
     145–46

Toxoplasma gondii,
    49–50
traveling, 152–54
tuna, 14

U
ultrasounds, 33–34
umbilical cord, 162

V
vinegar, 20
vitamin A, 23–24
vitamins, 21–24

W
water breaking, 123–25,
    126
water retention, 90–91
weight gain, 75–76
weight loss, 76–77
working, 155–57

X
x-rays, 32–33

Y
yeast infections, 64